ARS POETICA

OTHER VOLUMES OF GREEK AND ENGLISH POETRY
FROM COLENSO BOOKS

Sweet-voiced Sappho: Poems of Sappho and other Ancient Greek authors
translated into English verse by THEODORE STEPHANIDES,
with facing Greek text (2015)

The fruitful discontent of the word: a further selection of poems
by LAWRENCE DURRELL, edited by PETER BALDWIN (2018)
a supplement to Durrell's *Collected Poems 1931–1974*

Yannis Ritsos among his contemporaries: twentieth-century Greek poetry
by YANNIS RITSOS, GEORGE VAFOPOULOS, NIKOS GATSOS,
NIKIFOROS VRETTAKOS, MILTOS SACHTOURIS AND YANNIS KONDOS
translated by MARJORIE CHAMBERS (2018)

Στων Κυκλώπων τη Χώρα [In the land of the Cyclopes]
by IAKOVOS MENELAOU, in Greek only (2018)

Το Χρυσό Προσωπείο / The Golden Face
by THEODORE STEPHANIDES, Greek translation
by VERA KONIDARI with facing English text (2019)

Reading the signs
by JIM POTTS (2020)

Viral Verse: pandemic poems and images
by 16 contributors, edited by ANTHONY HIRST (2020)

Αρχαίου Κόσμου Ανείπωτα [Ancient World Untold]
by IAKOVOS MENELAOU in Greek only (2020)

Memorials, nightscapes, etcetera: poems of several decades
by ANTHONY HIRST (2020)

Ωδή στον Ήλιο Της [Ode to Her Sun]
by IAKOVOS MENELAOU in Greek only (2021)

Words on the table
by JIM POTTS (2021)

Poems by Daylight
by SARAH EKDAWI (2022)

Ειρήνη — Barış — Peace
by IAKOVOS MENELAOU, in Greek with Turkish translation
by EDA NUR İNCE and English translation by ANTHONY HIRST (2023)

*The Covid Years: a composite journal from many hands in poetry, prose
and pictures* by 26 contributors, edited by ANTHONY HIRST (2023),
including all the contents of *Viral Verse*

ANDONIS FOSTIERIS was born in Athens, Greece, in 1953. He studied Law at the University of Athens and History of Law at the Sorbonne. One of the younger poets of the Generation of the Seventies, Fostieris made his first appearance in 1971 at the age of eighteen with his collection *The Great Journey*. He was, already by 1975, the editor of *The New Poetry*, one of Greece's first new post-dictatorship journals. For thirty years (1981–2010) he was the co-editor and director of the esteemed literary journal $H\ \Lambda \acute{\varepsilon} \xi \eta$ (*The Word*). He has published ten collections, now all gathered together in *Complete Poems 1970–2020* which appeared in 2021.

After decades of the stifling domination of Modernism in Greece, Greek poetry, with Andonis Fostieris, returns to the ancient sources in order to move forward to the Post-modern — developing from, while surpassing Modernism. His poetics marks a change of direction and constitutes a new understanding of the role and function of contemporary poetry and its relationship to philosophy and tradition, while putting forward a coherent conceptualization of the function of language and its relation to truth.

Fostieris has been extensively translated into many languages, often by acclaimed translators. He has received many awards, most notably, in 2004, the Greek State Poetry prize for his 2003 collection *Precious Oblivion*, and in December 2010 the prestigious Ouranis Foundation Award of the Academy of Athens for his entire poetic oeuvre at that date.

ARS POETICA

POETRY WITHIN POETRY AND OTHER POEMS

BY

ANDONIS FOSTIERIS

GREEK TEXT WITH

FACING ENGLISH TRANSLATION

BY

IRENE LOULAKAKI-MOORE

EDITED BY

ANTHONY HIRST

COLENSO BOOKS
2023

First published June 2023
by
Colenso Books
68 Palatine Road London N16 8ST, UK
colensobooks@gmail.com

ISBN 978-1-912788-29-3

Greek text copyright © 2023
Andonis Fostieris (Ἀντώνης Φωστιέρης)

English translation, Introduction, Notes and Bibliography
copyright © 2023 Irene Loulakaki-Moore

The cover portrait of Andonis Fostieris (Ἀντώνης Φωστιέρης)
by Yannis Psychopedis (Γιάννης Ψυχοπαίδης)
is reproduced with their permission

ACKNOWLEDGEMENTS

I am very grateful to Andonis Fostieris for his help and encouragement throughout the many years of this project and for his careful checking of the final text. Conversations with him underlie every page of this book.

I am also greatly indebted to the editor, Anthony Hirst, for his collaboration in the final revision of the translations. His comments and insights have made this a better book.

Irene Loulakaki-Moore
May 2023

ΠΕΡΙΕΧΟΜΕΝΑ

Ἀπό ΤΟ ΜΕΓΑΛΟ ΤΑΞΙΔΙ (1971)
Καλόν ἐντάφιον ἡ ποίηση   2

Ἀπό ΣΚΟΤΕΙΝΟΣ ΕΡΩΤΑΣ (1977)
Τό μαῦρο   4
Ἐμπρηστικό ποίημα   6
Ποιός εἶσ᾽ ἐσύ   8
Ἔτσι περνοῦν   10
Μεταμόρφωση   12
Τό ποίημα   14
Ἡ παρακμή   16
Στούς κριτικούς   18

ΠΟΙΗΣΗ ΜΕΣ ΣΤΗΝ ΠΟΙΗΣΗ (1977): δεκαέξι ποιήματα   20

Ἀπό ΤΟ ΘΑ ΚΑΙ ΤΟ ΝΑ ΤΟΥ ΘΑΝΑΤΟΥ (1987)
Ὁ ἄσωτος   52
Ἀνεπίδεκτοι ἀθανασίας   54
Ὅτι τόν ποιητήν δέοι εἴπερ μέλλοι ποιητής εἶναι   56
Ὁ ἦχος τῶν λέξεων   58
Ὁ ἦχος τοῦ κόσμου   60
Γένεση   62

Ἀπό Η ΣΚΕΨΗ ΑΝΗΚΕΙ ΣΤΟ ΠΕΝΘΟΣ (1996)
Ἡ σκέψη ἀνήκει στό πένθος   64
Ποτάμι ποίημα   66
Ἐνώπιον ἀκροατηρίου   68
Μεταποίηση   72

Ἀπό ΠΟΛΥΤΙΜΗ ΛΗΘΗ (2003)
Ἡ ποίηση δέν γίνεται μέ ἰδέες   76
Κάθαρση   78
Ἀπό τό ποίημα βγαίνεις πάντα ζωντανός   80
Τά λόγια μένουν   84

Ἀπό ΤΟΠΙΑ ΤΟΥ ΤΙΠΟΤΑ (2013)
Τό γραπτό   88
Γράφω   90
Θέλω νά γράψω ἕνα ποίημα   92
Τό ἀπόβαρο   94
Τό κελί   96
Ἡ ποίηση   98
Τό ποίημα   100
Οἱ ποιητές   102
Μνημόσυνο γέννησης   104

CONTENTS

Introduction ... ix

From THE GREAT JOURNEY (1971)
Poetry is a noble shroud ... 3

From DARK EROS (1977)
The black ... 5
Fire poem ... 7
Who are you ... 9
And so they go by ... 11
Metamorphosis ... 13
The poem ... 15
Decadence ... 17
To the critics ... 19

POETRY WITHIN POETRY (1977): sixteen poems ... 21

From THE D AND A OF DEATH (1987)
The prodigal ... 53
Impervious to immortality ... 55
That the poet must if he would be a poet ... 57
The sound of words ... 59
The sound of the world ... 61
Genesis ... 63

From THOUGHT BELONGS TO MOURNING (1996)
Thought belongs to mourning ... 65
River poem ... 67
Before an audience ... 69
Metapoetry ... 73

From PRECIOUS OBLIVION (2003)
Poetry is not made with ideas ... 77
Purgation ... 79
You always emerge alive from a poem ... 81
The spoken words remain ... 85

From LANDSCAPES OF NOTHINGNESS (2013)
Writing ... 89
I write ... 91
I'd like to write a poem ... 93
The tare-weight ... 95
The cell ... 97
Poetry ... 99
The poem ... 101
The poets ... 103
Memorial of a birth ... 105

Notes ... 107
Bibliography ... 111

INTRODUCTION

BY

IRENE LOULAKAKI-MOORE

Le poème — cette hésitation prolongée entre le son et le sens
Paul Valéry[1]

> The Bibliography, which contains full details of all publications cited in the footnotes, will be found at the end of the book. It is placed there (rather than immediately after this Introduction) because it also serves for the Notes which immediately precede it. (Editor)

According to James Holmes' "Two-map Model of Translation Process" the translator of a work receives the source-text and forms in her mind a "map", a mental representation that is actually the basis for the act of translation and guides the translator's choice on the level of structure, lexis and context. This map is a reading, a subjective construction, conditioned by the translator's pre-existing knowledge, beliefs and expectations that lead her to concentrate on certain components of the poem and ignore others during the process of transference and the production of the target-text.[2]

The fifty-eight poem translations which you have in your hands are the fruit of nearly eight years of looking at and correcting these maps of translation in an attempt to minimize the risk of them becoming "maps of misreading".[3] During these years I was also studying the poetry of Fostieris[4] and had the privilege to work closely with the poet on these maps, trying to identify any misconceptions that might throw an innocent reader's boat onto the rocks instead of leading it into a safe harbour. During this collaboration I discovered the poet's obsession with detail and accuracy, and that has been both a compass and a storm lantern for me. Like Mallarmé,[5] Fostieris leaves nothing to chance: poetry is for him a precise art where even ambiguity and polysemy are carefully employed as integral parts of the whole. Luckily, the control the poet has over his

---

[1] Valéry 1960, 636. Quoted below in English on pages x and xx.
[2] See Loulakaki-Moore 2010a, 15–19; Holmes 1988, 81–84; Beaugrade 1978, 25.
[3] I am referring here to Harold Bloom 1975, *A Map of Misreading,* which concerns the then-recent poets' Freudian and antagonistic reading of the poets who had influenced them.
[4] See Loulakaki-Moore 2010b, 2013, 2014, 2018a, 2018b.
[5] "The order of a book of poems breaks through innate or universal, eliminating chance" (Mallarmé, cited in Lloyd 1999, 55).

medium never became a stifling hold on the translator. Although he speaks English and often discussed with me alternative solutions, he was happy just to give me the clear co-ordinates of his poem-islands, leaving the navigation to me.

The whole venture begun from a list of poems of poetics that I made under Fostieris' guidance as part of the research for a paper I was writing back in 2014.[6] That is when I realized the significance that poetry about poetry has for Fostieris and his generation and how, for him, *ars poetica* is not just a manual but also a source of inspiration.

The poems in the present volume appear in the order they have in his collected edition of 2021.[7] The title of this present anthology, *Ars Poetica*, and its subtitle, *Poetry within Poetry*, are also a product of my cooperation with the poet and it reflects Fostieris' lifelong preoccupation with what Paul Valéry described as "the prolonged hesitation between sound and meaning", a relationship that I will analyze below, relating it to Roman Jakobson's seminal essay "Linguistics and Poetics".[8]

During the process of translation, I was often overwhelmed by the precise way Fostieris combines sounds to form syllables and syllables to create words and lines. Thus, I avoided altogether poems like Ἡ ὁμιλία ("Speech") in which the title noun *omilia* is echoed in the punch line in the homophone *omi leia* (ὠμὴ λεία, "raw plunder"). At other points I had to reconcile myself with loss, as in "Writing" (page 89), where no exact equivalent exists to preserve the highly charged near-identity of the words γραπτό (*grapto*, "writing" or "something written") and γραφτό (*graphto*, a variant spelling of *grapto*, which can also mean "fate"). Eventually I settled on "writing" for *grapto* and "what has been written" for *graphto* . Then, in "Fire Poem" (page 7), the reversal of syllables in two hyphenated words in the first line of the original, Τάφοι-φυτά (*Taphi-phita*) is lost in the translation "sepulchral saplings", as is the rhyme created in "Decadence" (page 17) by the encapsulation of one verb *liosei* (λιώσει, "melted") in another *teleiosei* (τελειώσει,"finished").

My overarching concern was to preserve in translation the way prosody and typographical layout contribute to the meaning of the original. This is evident, as I have tried to convey in translation, in the very first poem of the collection, and the only one written in strict rhyme, "Poetry is a noble shroud" (page 3), as it is in many of the poems in the sequence "Poetry within poetry" (pages 21–51) which constitute extremely condensed samples of Fostieris' favourite themes and craftsmanship.

Elsewhere there have been quite a few propitious instances, as in "To

---

[6] Loulakaki-Moore 2014.

[7] The Contents list on page vii shows which of Fostieris' ten collections each poem in the book belongs to, though not all ten collections are represented.

[8] Jakobson 1981. For Valéry's original French see the epigraph on page ix.

the critics" (page 19) where the sound repetition of the original /st/ and /ch/: *I stichoi / Eine ta stachia pou therisan / Elissomenes meres* (Οἱ στίχοι / Εἶναι τὰ στάχυα ποὺ θέρισαν / Ἑλισσόμενες μέρες) is recreated through the repetition of the sound /r/: "The lines / Are the crops reaped/ by rotating days". In "The tare-weight" (page 95) the irony suggested by *phoni* / *phonien* (φωνή / φωνῆεν) and *symphonei* / *symphono* (συμφωνεῖ / σύμφωνο) is fortuitously conveyed without straying far from a faithful translation by "voice" / "vowel" and "consonant" / "consent" respectively.

With poems like "Purgation" (page 79) where the word choice in the original is guided by the chiming effect and not so much by the words' denotative or connotative meaning, I have taken more liberties in order to recreate it in English, replacing the pairs *kardies — bradies* (καρδιές — βραδιές, "hearts — evenings") and *cheria — macheria* (χέρια — μαχαίρια, "hands — knives") with the comparable "hearts — darts" and "lives — knives". I have taken equally bold decisions in "Metapoetry" (pages 73, 75) where originality in poetry is examined. The poem contains fragments of Empedocles and Heraclitus in ancient Greek. To convey the macaronic effect I rendered those in slightly archaic English. In some poems where we have single words or phrases quoting or alluding to older texts, I chose a translator's easy way out, using endnotes so as not to disrupt the flow of the poem.

Although Fostieris has been translated into English before, notably by Kimon Friar, as early as 1984,[9] this is the first translation of his poems which has the character of a thematic anthology, and which may also be regarded as a poetic manifesto, as the title, *Ars Poetica*, suggests. Fostieris, being completely dedicated to poetry, is not one of those poets who also support their art with their lecturing, essay-writing or criticism. His view of the world, language and art is all encapsulated in his poetry in a dense and often playful manner as the analysis that follows aims to show.

Employing Roman Jakobson's terms, we could say that the relation between linguistics and poetics constitutes an inextricable source of inspiration for Fostieris. Jakobson's exploration of poetics in relation to other forms of verbal behaviour begins from the question: "What makes a verbal message a work of art?" And this leads him to his famous six-factor communication model and to the conclusion that "the poetic function projects the principle of equivalence from the axis of selection into the axis of combination."[10] According to Jakobson, during any kind of verbal act, the speaker chooses his words from the axis of selection on the basis of equivalence, synonymity and antonymity, in order to build up a sequence on the axis of combination. The former axis being the vertical axis of

---

[9] Fostieris 1984; see also Fostieris 2009.
[10] The essay "Linguistics and poetics" which introduces the six-factor communication model is largely an essay on versification (Jakobson 1981, 27).

language as a whole (*langue*) that exists somewhere in space, as a virtual object, a mental representation, a "simulacrum" as Barthes would call it,[11] and the latter being the horizontal axis of speech (*parole*) as it unfolds in time. The vertical axis is characterized as something fixed, although constructed, whereas the horizontal one is characterized by change, depending on the way related signifiers combine in time in order to produce meaning.[12] As Jakobson is quick to admit, this equivalence between the sounds of words and their meaning is not just a poetic but a metalingual function as well: it occurs when we use equivalent units, synonyms, to explain a word. Jakobson's definition at this point opens up the space in which to question the stability of the relationship between signified and signifier.[13] Is it a fixed and unshakeable relationship common to all users of a language system or can it be contaminated by the intentions of the speaker and/or the listener? This is exactly the space that deconstruction came to challenge in the late 1960s and early 1970s and that Fostieris creatively exploits in the poems in this volume. Fostieris seems to be constantly preoccupied with the axis of combination, the way sounds combine to form syllables and syllables in turn combine to form words and phrases. This explains his predilection for metaphors of the poem as a forward-moving noisy construction, as in "The poem" (page 15):

> What could a dog be, or a worm
>   or a poem
> That moves forward
>   with whistles and bangs?
>
> Burning words it crosses steppes
>   — And then?

In the above excerpt and also in "Fire Poem" (page 7) poetry is depicted as a mechanism, an engine that burns words as fuel in order to function:

> I defy for my part my decay
> I defy my decay now inflamed
> Burning
> The yellow leaves of old poets

---

[11] According to Barthes (1972, 210) "the simulacrum is intellect added to the object", a creation of the intellect and imagination, a "veritable fabrication" that resembles the real world in order to make it intelligible.

[12] Jakobson's axes of selection and combination correspond to Saussure's paradigmatic and syntagmatic modes of arrangement in verbal behaviour. (Jacobson 1985, 146).

[13] "[E]very linguistic unit is bipartite and involves both aspects — one sensible and the other intelligible, or in other words, both the *signans*, 'signifier' (Saussure's *signifiant*) and the *signatum*, 'signified' (*signifié*)" (Jakobson 1949, 6).

> And whatever else I loved
> In the first period of hatred.
> […]
> I say: Let's open the valve
> And let our intoxicated lines become the fuse
> For a blaze in the illegal hangouts
> Inside the venomous skyscrapers of the intellect.

As I have shown elsewhere, for Fostieris Heraclitus' ever-living fire is a metonymy for the act of writing itself.[14] But the *logos* that permeates his poems is not Eliot's Pentecostal Fire that turns the poet into a prophet uttering universal truths,[15] as we can see in "Notes for tomorrow" (1987):

> Set fire to poems, burn words, shoo away the greedy
>   snake that's coming. And that's hissing.[16]

The speaker "burns words" like wood, to produce a temporal effect, demystifying the metaphysical correspondence between words and concepts, the signifier (the sound image) and the signified. By doing so he subverts the modernist quest for the eternal behind the ephemeral, the soul behind the body, the spiritual behind the material.[17] The poet is on a mission to keep his readers alert, reminding them that they are on a construction site: language is not a set of a-temporal concepts that exist somewhere in space but a set of forward-progressing associations of sounds that take place in time. Where a modernist would make wild jumps from the now into the eternal, in the poetry of Fostieris we find the opposite move: the concept generates the sound, the relationship between signified and signifier becomes metalingual, it stops being metaphoric and mystifying. By abolishing the binary relation between signified and signifier he erases the metaphysical space where *langue* exists from the beginning of time in an ideal state, as in a treasury. For him language is currency that has lost its value, silver that cannot be redeemed. In "Decadence" (page 17), there is no transcendental counterpart to the sound of words:

> If I write poems it's because I know

---

[14] Loulakaki-Moore 2014, 107–113.
[15] As scholars agree, "When Heraclitus spoke of 'god' or the 'divine', he clearly had in mind the Logos-fire" (Guthrie 1962, 472). As Derrida remarks (1997, 10): "All the metaphysical determinations of truth, and even the one beyond metaphysical onto-theology that Heidegger reminds us of, are more or less immediately inseparable from the instance of logos."
[16] Fostieris 2021, 200; first collected in Fostieris 1987; not included in the present volume.
[17] Modernism's quest for such correspondence was first proclaimed in 1859 in Baudelaire's essay on the painter Constantin Guys (Loulakaki-Moore 2014, 93).

> All the alphabets in the world have melted
> All the words and all the lines are finished
> The days' maimed limbs kicking at my door
> Their rabid slobber their brittle laughter
>   And the poems
> The silverware I will not sell
>   — Who would buy it?

Similarly in "The tare-weight" (page 95):

> You speak with words.
> You translate the unknown
> Into something more unknown. Exchanging
> The unliftable weight of matter
> For a forged portfolio
> Full of immaterial assets, participles
> Pronouns
> And verbs.
> [...]   Changing
> Outside of language and thought
> The unknown
> Into something more tenebrous.
> And unliftable.
>
> Into the immaterial
> Tare-weight
> Of matter.

From 1977 up to his most recent collection of 2020, the poet is concerned with the axis of grammar, putting continuously in question the process of signification itself. In the following excerpts, the first from "That the poet must if he would be a poet" (page 57) and the second from "The tare-weight" again, the only undeniable thing in language is sound and the organs of its production:

> The splash of surf generates the sea and behold the voice
> Creates a larynx which speaks. Alas;
> The carpenter is no carpenter without his wood [...].

> Which chthonic larynx
> Gives voice to a vowel?

The speaker keeps drawing our attention to the way phonemes are combined to create sound-images of things: the words. These images are the tare-weight of matter, since it is through words that the objective world (here the sea, the earth) transforms into anti-matter. The irony here lies in the fact that the poet acknowledges the word, the signifier, as the immaterial counterpart of reality but dispenses with the transcendental signified as of no consequence. Language has been shown to work no magic, as in "Impervious to Immortality" (page 55):

> Since, as I know, the formula doesn't yet exist
> To concoct a lasting moment.

Realizations like these challenge the modernists head-on. One cannot help but think of Seferis who, as a poet/mystic, sought to capture in his poetry the eternal, absolute truth in a visionary moment, "in and out of time".[18] By challenging the transcendental counterpart of words Fostieris denounces the mystical path to knowledge and the modernist role of the poet as a prophet, as in "Who are you" (page 9):

> How come I am unable
> In the years of my hours
> To align myself with a beautiful lie [...].

In "To the critics" (page 19) verses catch fire as "they head off / To the dreamlike blue yonder", while the speaker sombrely acknowledges that he seems to speak a "dead language". It is a language that refuses to construct the consolatory "other realities" of which Lyotard writes.[19] If Elytis employed the Christian language in order to displace Christ and even the God of Genesis by appropriating his creative power to determine by utterance,[20] Fostieris, in his poem "Genesis" (page 63), does the same, to underline the subjectivity of such statements:

> I said "darkness" and behold there
> Was the earth with its plants its animals
> Invisible immense and delicate
> And in my likeness.

---

[18] This ideal of the self-legislating artist, who seeks to recreate this process in the literary act was described by Seferis as the struggle of the poet "to be able to say, 'Let there be light', and for there to be light" (1964), cited in Beaton 1987, 148. Then there are Seferis' lines, from "The mood of a day", "Where is love that with one stroke / cuts time in two and stuns it?" and *Erotikos Logos* 5, "Where is the double-edged day that had changed everything?" (Seferis 1995, 239 and 252; for the original Greek, see Seferis 1974, 17 and 32).

[19] "Modernity, in whatever age it appears, cannot exist without a shattering of belief and without discovery of the 'lack of reality', together with the invention of other realities" (Lyotard 1992, 146). In his Nobel acceptance speech Elytis states (1987, 118) that he perceives the Heraclitan logos as the "second reality [...] the world within this world" that people fail to grasp.

[20] See the discussion in Hirst 2004, especially pages 357–358.

To Elytis' solar metaphysics Fostieris responds dynamically with a metaphysics of darkness.[21] He places the artist back in the cosmos, subject to the same deceptions and epistemological restrictions as everybody else.[22]

In "The sound of words" (page 59) and "The sound of the world" (page 61), the speaker, in his struggle to find a tangible relation between the words and the world, between signifier and signified, finds only the arbitrariness of the sign and its distance from the real world. He realizes the materiality of language: his words are "made of wood",[23] and, like Lautréamont,[24] he addresses his Muse in second person singular and in imperatives, not asking her to speak to him but ordering her to listen[25] to the sound of the cosmos which is not music but a "screech", a "roaring" and a "drone".

"Before an audience"(pages 69, 71) is another shrewd exploration of the fluidity of language, inspiration and reception. Here the speaker is very ironic regarding the poet's quest for universal truths from the perspective of the eternal, *sub specie aeternitatis*. Behind this quest, he finds nothing but the poet's vanity and the mutability of sign:

> That indeed is an audience!
> With words flowing in its bones,
> Wavering
> With the instability of the signified. Inspiration
> Was rippling its skin into wrinkles
> And the seabed and the bellowing surface
> In the darkness were one.

Apart from re-grounding the poet in the cosmos, the above poem also constitutes a comment on the ethical character of such a quest in art. As Wittgenstein notes:

---

[21] I use the term "metaphysics" here as it is defined by contemporary philosophers as an impossible enterprise, doomed by the inability of the rational mind to provide a safe answer to the grand metaphysical questions. See McGinn 1993 and Thomasson 2009.

[22] I have noted elsewhere (Loulakaki 2014) how Fostieris employs the philosophy of Heraclitus in order to show how subjectivity distorts reality.

[23] The expression ξύλινη γλώσσα ("wooden language") signifies pretention and was imported into Greek from the French "langue de bois", in the second half of the twentieth century in order to denote the hollow language of authority.

[24] Interestingly, Fostieris translated some of Lautréamont's poems for the first issue of Ἡ Λέξη, a journal he co-edited (Lautréamont 1981).

[25] The ambivalence of the poet's invocation of the Muse even in Antiquity has often been remarked. "What does it mean for a poet to invoke a Muse? When Homer calls on the goddess to 'sing the wrath of Achilles' is that a command or a request?" (Murray 2002, 38).

> The work of art is the object seen *sub specie aeternitatis*, and the good life is the world seen *sub specie aeternitatis*. This is the connection between art and ethics. The usual way of looking at things sees objects as it were from the midst of them, the view *sub specie aeternitatis* from outside. [26]

In the twin poems "Purgation" (page 79) and "You always emerge alive from a poem", (pages 81, 83), the distance between the reality of the poem and the real world is emphasized. The tone of the first poem is conversational and the reality of the poem is called "a forgery", while in the second poem the "elsewhere" is the real world and not a second reality, not a promised land:

> No actuality
> Will actually endorse
> Such a forgery.
> No alliteration
> Reiterates the facts.

> A dead body inside a poem
> Doesn't strike you as wrong. On the contrary.
> [...]
> When elsewhere
> (Again you get why we say "elsewhere")
> Blood is spilled
> Blood freezes
> Blood forms clots
> (Reality, you see,
> cannot make beautiful lines)
> And metastases triumph
> With high-jumps
> Into the depths.

The dead body inside the poem points to Karyotakis, who famously committed suicide, marking a whole generation of poets; and "ailments/ That lie in fantasy / And words" points to Cavafy, who notably equated poetry with medicine.[27] In these twin poems Fostieris brings out the tensions between rhetoric and grammar, between metaphor and metonymy. Metaphor is a poetic lie and it is always at odds with predication, which is a truth claim, a reference. The dead body in the poem is not what Harold Bloom would call the *apophrades*, his last revisionary ratio where the

[26] Wittgenstein 1953, 683.
[27] See the Note to this poem on page 109.

dead return and

> the poem is now *held* open to the precursor, where once it *was* open and the uncanny effect is that the new poem's achievement makes it seem to us, not as though the precursor were writing it, but as though the later poet himself had written the precursor's characteristic work.[28]

The presence of the precursor in the poem exists side by side with medical vocabulary, like a corpse inside a morgue.

In "That the poet must if would be a poet" (page 57), Fostieris regrets that poetry is still governed by prescriptions like the one accepted even by Socrates in Plato's *Phaedo*: "That the poet must if he would be a poet compose fables but not speeches."[29] With the same move he takes up Valéry's belief that the first line is given by the gods,[30] and, turning to the readers, he instructs them to borrow the first line:

> That's why I tell you:
> Grab a pen, get paper and begin —
> If the gods don't grant you the first line, borrow it:
>
> The splash of surf generates the sea and behold the voice

In this excerpt we witness Fostieris' poetry and *ars poetica* at work. The last line above, which is also the last line of the poem (and a repetition of the first line) does not end with a full stop. It is left hanging there, suspended in the air, offered to the reader to borrow, flouting the conventions of writing, and closer to its origin in the voice, *phoni* (φωνή). As Derrida, following Aristotle, contends, all signifiers, first and foremost written signifiers, the words, are derivative:

> [I]t is because the voice, producer of *the first symbols*, has a relationship of essential and immediate proximity with the mind. Producer of the first signifier, it is not just a simple signifier among others. It signifies "mental experiences" which themselves reflect or mirror things by natural resemblance. Between being and mind, things and feelings, there would be a relationship of translation of natural signification; between mind and logos, a relationship of conventional symbolization. And the *first* convention, which would relate immediately to the order of natural and universal

---

[28] Bloom 1997, 16 (emphases in the original).
[29] See Notes, page 107.
[30] "Les dieux, gracieusement, nous donnent pour rien tel premier vers" (Valéry 1957, 482).

signification, would be produced as spoken language.[31]

If Fostieris draws the reader's attention to the alphabet, its sounds and the processes of syllabification, reading and writing, in other words to the "materiality of the text" and the "mechanisms of writing",[32] it is because, like many poets of his generation, he is suspicious of the ways in which vocabularies create descriptions of the world and ourselves, instead of adequately or inadequately expressing them.[33] The socio-political, economic and intellectual developments in Greece and elsewhere in the 1970s rendered obsolete previous generations' search for the "lost centre" and the grand narratives that validate it. Unlike the Modernist poet-authority, Fostieris, does not stand in the centre of his creation, like a unique owner of truth and sole creator of meaning. By bringing out the tension between the poetic and the metalingual function in his poems, he activates the signifying chain, the play of signification,[34] inviting the reader to an interactive game of completion of meaning. The inherent self-criticism of his poems opens the way to pluralistic interpretation.

I have discussed elsewhere the way in which Fostieris' poetics surpasses Modernism and marks a turn towards the Post-modern, constituting a new approach to the role and function of contemporary poetry, while it also proposes a coherent conceptualization of the role of language and its relation to the truth.[35] Poets of previous generations who continued writing well into the 1970s and '80s noticed the change and even responded to it creatively.[36] It was critical — and especially conservative academic — reception that downplayed the change. One could say that

---

[31] Derrida 1997, 11. This is Derrida's elaboration of Aristotle's contention (*De interpretatione*, 1, 16a 3) that spoken words (τὰ ἐν τῇ φωνῇ) are the symbols of mental experience (τῶν ἐν τῇ ψυχῇ παθημάτων σύμβολα) and written words are the symbols of spoken words (τὰ γραφόμενα τῶν ἐν τῇ φωνῇ).
[32] Van Dyck 1988, 95.
[33] For the way conceptions are made by our vocabularies see Rorty 1989, 7. For the way this is related to Heraclitus in Fostieris' poetry see Loulakaki 2014.
[34] As Derrida has convincingly shown (1980, 278–294), by giving a structure a centre, a fixed origin, one organizes the structure, while at the same time limiting or even closing off the *freeplay* which a structure opens up and makes possible.
[35] Loulakaki-Moore 2013, 2014, 2018a and 2018b.
[36] Elytis declares (1987, 42) that poetry begins from the point when death no longer has the last word. The poetry of Fostieris begins from the opposite pole as the titles of many of his collections reveal: *Dark Eros* (1977), *The Devil Sang in Tune* (1981, translation 1984), *The D and A of Death* (1987), *Thought Belongs to Mourning* (1996), *Precious Oblivion* (2003, translation 2009), *Landscapes of Nothingness* (2013) and *Second Death* (2020). Elytis' increasing preoccupation with the philosophical issues of existence and mortality in the collections published after 1978 are very revealing, in the light of such opposing viewpoints.

Fostieris and the poets of his Generation attempted what Surrealism (another avant-garde movement which met with a great deal of resistance in Greece) had attempted: the secularization of inspiration. In his article "Surrealism: the Last Snapshot of the European Intelligentsia", Walter Benjamin notes how the writings of the Surrealists are concerned "with experiences, not with theories and still less with phantasms" and goes on to praise Surrealism's attempt to secularize inspiration, to overcome religious illumination and to create "a profane illumination" (*profane Erleuchtung*), a materialistic, anthropological inspiration.[37] The transformation of inspiration after the Surrealists made available for everyone what had been the privilege of the poet-initiate, in line with Lautréamont's injunction: "Poetry should be made by everyone. Not just by one."[38]

With his "prolonged hesitation between sound and meaning" Fostieris wants to bring the written word closer to the mental experience, the feeling or the thing in itself. He does not deny the referential function of language, he only exhibits his suspiciousness twoards the authority that says, "my language is true". By doing so he cleverly abstains from imposing on the readers his version of meaning, inviting them instead to join in the game of signification. But because signification is a dynamic, ongoing process, Nietzsche warns us that "To imprint upon becoming the character of being — that is the supreme will to power".[39] One might ask here whether the invitation to the reader to join in the game of signification signals the end of what Bloom would call "strong poets"? The fact that the speaking subject invites pluralistic interpretations does not mean that he is no longer the controlling subject of his writings, while translations are living proof of the multiple meanings behind a signifier.

---

[37] Benjamin 1978, 179.
[38] Lautréamont 1990, 356. For a discussion, see Chrysanthopoulos 2012, 304.
[39] Nietzsche 1968, 330.

ARS POETICA

ΚΑΛΟΝ ΕΝΤΑΦΙΟΝ Η ΠΟΙΗΣΗ

Στούς προσφιλεῖς νεκρούς ἡ Ποίηση κάνει λαμπρή κηδεία.
Μ'ἐπισημότητα καί μ'αἴγλη μυθική
Βαθιά τούς θάβει. Χαιρετάει μέ μουσική
Τούς ρίχνει στέφανα, μιά πλάκα κρύα,

Πίσω τῶν στίχων ἡ ἀτέλειωτη πομπή
Κι ἀπάνω μιά ἐπιτύμβια Ἱστορία.

Ἀγγέλων χοῦφτες τούς σφραγίζουν τή σιωπή
Μέχρι τή Δεύτερή τους Παρουσία
Πού μέ συντρίμμια τήν ταφόπλακα οἱ νεκροί
Τό νοτισμένο θά κινήσουνε κορμί

Κάποιες ασύνορες αφήνοντας πατρίδες
Ὡριμασμένη να μᾶς δρέψουν τήν ζωή.

Ἀναστημένες οἱ νεκρές μας οἱ ἐλπίδες
Μέ νέα δύναμη γιγάντια, νέα ὁρμή,
Τά χέρια γύρω ἀπ'τό λαιμό μας θά τυλίξουν,

Ἐκδικητές, τυραννοκτόνοι, νά μᾶς πνίξουν.

POETRY IS A NOBLE SHROUD

Poetry grants illustrious funeral to the beloved dead.
With solemnity and fabled glory
Laying them below. With music salutatory
It lays wreaths, a cold slab,

Behind the lines the endless procession
And a sepulchral History above.

Hands of angels seal their silence
Until their Second Coming
When the dead, the gravestone shattered
Will move their sodden bodies

Borderless homelands left behind
So as to reap our ripened life.

Our dead hopes raised again
With fresh strength of giants, fresh momentum,
Around our necks they'll wrap their claws,

Avengers, tyrannicides, to strangle us.

ΤΟ ΜΑΥΡΟ

Τό μαῦρο εἶν᾽ οἱ λέξεις
Πού πέσανε ἡ μιά πάνω στήν ἄλλη
Τά τυπωμένα ποιήματα
Τό ἕνα πάνω στ᾽ ἄλλο
Κι ὅλα τά χρώματα πού ζήτησαν ἐκεῖ
Τό τελικό κρησφύγετο.

THE BLACK

The black is the words
That fell one upon the other
The printed poems
One upon the other
And all the colours that sought there
Their final refuge.

ΕΜΠΡΗΣΤΙΚΟ ΠΟΙΗΜΑ

Τάφοι-φυτά πού φυτρώνουνε μέσα μου
Καί περιμένω τόν καιρό πού θά καρποφορήσουν·
Ὅ,τι ρουφάει ἡ ζαρωμένη ρίζα τους
Στίς σπηλιές καί στίς λάσπες τοῦ νοῦ μου.

Προκαλῶ τή φθορά μου κι ἐγώ
Προκαλῶ τή φθορά μου καιγόμενος
Καίγοντας
Κίτρινα φύλλα παλιῶν ποιητῶν
Κι ὅ,τι ἄλλο ἀγάπησα
Στήν πρώτη περίοδο τοῦ μίσους.

Ἄκου βαθιά τή φωνή τῶν φλεβῶν μας·
Σφαῖρες κυκλοφοροῦν στό αἷμα
Κι ἐκπυρσοκροτήσεις σ'ἕνα μέλλον ἄδηλο
Πού σφίγγεται πίσω ἀπ'τά κάγκελα τοῦ θυμωμένου χρόνου.
Λέω: ν'ἀνοίξουμε τή στρόφιγγα
Κι οἱ μεθυσμένοι στίχοι μας νά γίνουν τό στουπί
Γιά μιά πυρκαϊά στά παράνομα στέκια
Στούς δηλητηριώδεις οὐρανοξύστες τοῦ πνεύματος.

FIRE POEM

Sepulchral saplings grow inside me
And I wait for the time of their fruition;
Whatever their crinkled roots are suckling
Inside the hollows and mire of my mind.

I defy for my part my decay
I defy my decay now inflamed
Burning
The yellow leaves of old poets
And whatever else I loved
In the first period of hatred.

Hear deep down the voice in our veins;
Bullets circulate in the blood
And explosions in a doubtful future
Which is cowering behind the bars of enraged time.
I say: Let's open the valve
And let our intoxicated lines become the fuse
For a blaze in the illegal hangouts
Inside the venomous skyscrapers of the intellect.

ΠΟΙΟΣ ΕΙΣ' ΕΣΥ

Ποιός εἶσ' ἐσύ
Πού περπατᾶς πάνω στήν κόψη τῶν ποιημάτων μου
Ἀνοίγοντας τή μουσική στά δυό
Γιά νά χωρέσεις
Γιά νά σηκώσεις μιά σημαία δυσανάλογη
Πάνω στή σφαίρα μιᾶς ζωῆς πού δέ σοῦ ἀνήκει·
Ποιός εἶσ' ἐσύ
Ἐσύ
Πού γνώρισες τό φύλλο τό χλωρό
Κάτω ἀπ' τόν ἥλιο πρίν αἰῶνες
Πού ἀνάσανες τόσο σκοτάδι
Γιά τό μέλλον σου.

Ποτέ σου δέ μοῦ δόθηκες
Καί δέ θά σοῦ δοθῶ
Καθώς σέ μένα τίποτα δέ δόθηκε
— Κι οὔτε μποροῦσε νά δοθεῖ
Ἀκόμη κι ἄν ὑπῆρξε.

Τόσα πηγάδια, τόσες μέρες
— Πῶς δέ γέμισαν! —
Τόση ὀμορφιά, τόσες παγίδες
— Πῶς μοῦ ξέφυγαν! —
Πῶς δέν μπορῶ
Μέσα στά χρόνια τῶν ὡρῶν μου
Νά συνταχτῶ μ' ἕνα ὡραῖο ψέμα,
Καί κινδυνεύω σ' ἕναν κόσμο πού δέν ξέρω
Σέ μιά ἑτοιμόγεννη ἐποχή πού μέ παραμονεύει.

WHO ARE YOU

Who are you
Who walk on the edge of my poems
Cleaving the music in two
In order to make room
To raise a flag out of all proportion
On the sphere of a life that's not yours;
Who are you
You
Who came to know the green leaf
Ages ago beneath the sun
Who breathed in so much darkness
For your years to come.

You never gave yourself to me
And I'll never give myself to you
Just as nothing was given to me
— And it couldn't have been given
Even if it had existed.

So many wells, so many days
— How come they didn't fill up! —
So much beauty, so many snares
— How come they got away from me! —
How come I am unable
In the years of my hours
To align myself with a beautiful lie,
And I'm in peril in a world I don't know
In a season in labour waiting to ambush me.

ΕΤΣΙ ΠΕΡΝΟΥΝ

Ποιός εἶπε οἱ ἐποχές περνοῦν οἱ ἐποχές ἔρχονται
Οἱ ἐποχές ἡ μιά μέ ρίζες στήν καρδιά τῆς ἄλλης
Ποιός περπατάει σ' αὐτό τό ποίημα ποιός τό διάβασε
Καί ποιός μετά ἀπό χρόνια σ' ἄλλην ἐποχή
Θά τό διαβάσει
    Ποιός
Στήν ἤρεμη ἔρημο τήν ἄγρια ἔρημο
Ποιός ξέρει τώρα κάποτε πώς ἴσως τό διαβάσει
    Ποιός.

AND SO THEY GO BY

Who said seasons go seasons come
Seasons rooted in one another's hearts
Who walks in this poem who reads it
And who years later at another season
Will read it
        Who
In the serene desert in the savage desert
Who knows now whether one day they may read it
        Who.

ΜΕΤΑΜΟΡΦΩΣΗ

Κάποτε θά πάψω νά μιλῶ.

Τά χέρια μου θά γίνουνε κλαριά
Τά μάτια μου θά γίνουνε λυχνάρια
Οἱ σκέψεις μου θά γίνουνε φτερά
Τό στόμα μου ἅ τό στόμα μου
Θά πλημμυρίσει
Θά μουσκέψει
Τά ποιήματα.

METAMORPHOSIS

Sometime I will cease to speak.

My arms become branches
My eyes become lamps
My thoughts become wings
My mouth, ah my mouth
Will overflow
Will drench
The poems.

ΤΟ ΠΟΙΗΜΑ

Τά πράγματα μουσκέψαν ἀπ' τό φῶς
Ποτίστηκαν ὥς τό βαθύ μεδούλι
Πρήζονται
Μέσα στόν πιό λαμπρό τους θάνατο.

Γλυκό μου πλάσμα
Τί θά πεῖ «γλυκό»
Καί τί θά πεῖ «θά πεῖ»
Καί τί «καί τί»;

Σ' αὐτόν τόν κόσμο πού βυθίζεται στό φῶς
Τί νά 'ναι φῶς
Τί νά 'ναι σκύλος τί σκουλήκι
                         τί ἕνα ποίημα
Πού προχωράει
              μέ σφυρίγματα καί κρότους;

Καίγοντας λέξεις διασχίζει στέπες
    — Κι ἔπειτα;

Καπνοί κι οὐράνιες τουλίπες στόν ἀέρα
    — Καί λοιπόν;

Γλυκό μου ποίημα πού δακρύζεις
Καί πού ὑγραίνεσαι
Σέ ἀγαπῶ καί σέ προδίνω
Καί σέ ἐχθρεύομαι
Εἶσαι τό ἀκοίμητο σκοτάδι πού μέ ἀνάστησε
Εἶμαι τό ἀντίστοιχο
Τοῦ πιό κρυφοῦ σου
στίχου.

THE POEM

Things are sodden with light
Steeped to the deep marrow
Swollen
Within their most brilliant death.

My sweet creature
What does "sweet" mean
And what does "mean" mean
And what "and what"?

In this world sinking into the light
What could light possibly be
What could a dog be, or a worm
                              or a poem
That moves forward
                with whistles and bangs?

Burning up words it crosses steppes
    — And then?

Smoke and heavenly tulips in the air
    — And what then?

My sweet poem you're weeping
And wetting yourself
I love you and I betray you
And I'm your enemy
You are the sleepless dark that raised me
I am the counterpart
Of your most veiled
line.

Η ΠΑΡΑΚΜΗ

Ἄν γράφω ποιήματα εἶναι γιατί τό ξέρω
Ὅλα τ' ἀλφάβητα τοῦ κόσμου ἔχουνε λιώσει
Ὅλες οἱ λέξεις κι ὅλ' οἱ στίχοι ἔχουν τελειώσει
Οἱ μέρες τό κουτσό τους πόδι μοῦ χτυπάει τήν πόρτα
Τό λυσσασμένο σάλιο τους τό γυάλινό τους γέλιο
    Καί τά ποιήματα
Τ' ἀσημικό πού δέ θά τό πουλήσω
      — Ποιός τ' ἀγόραζε; —
         Μιά προδομένη ὑπόθεση λοιπόν
         Μιά πλήρης ἧττα.

DECADENCE

If I write poems it's because I know
All the alphabets in the world have melted
All the words and all the lines are finished
The days' maimed limbs kicking at my door
Their rabid slobber, their brittle laughter
     And the poems
The silverware I will not sell
       — Who would buy it? —
         A dead loss then
         An absolute debacle.

ΣΤΟΥΣ ΚΡΙΤΙΚΟΥΣ

Ἡ ποίηση ἀπαντάει στούς κριτικούς μέ ποίηση
Ὅπως ἡ φύση στούς σοφούς σά φύση,
Κι ἕνα τεράστιο κύμα ἀδιαφορίας καβαλάει τά κράσπεδα
Σαρώνοντας τίς πολιτεῖες ἀπ' τούς μάταιους στίχους.

Ἄλλοτε λέω:
Οἱ στίχοι
Εἶναι τά στάχυα πού θέρισαν
Ἑλισσόμενες μέρες
Καί παίρνοντας φωτιά ξεκίνησαν
Σ' ὀνειρώδη οὐρανό.

Λυπᾶμαι
Πού μᾶλλον μιλάω
Μιά γλώσσα νεκρή.
Δέν πιστεύω βεβαίως σέ ἀνάσταση·
Πιστεύω
Ἐντούτοις
Μέ πάθος
Στό
Θάνατο.

TO THE CRITICS

Poetry responds to the critics with poetry
As nature responds to the learned as nature,
And a vast wave of indifference mounts the kerbs
Clearing the towns of the vain lines of verse.

Sometimes I say:
The lines
Are the crops reaped
By revolving days
And catching fire they head off
To the dreamlike blue yonder.

I'm sad
That I seem to speak
A dead language.
For sure I don't believe in resurrection;
I believe
However
Passionately
In
Death.

ΠΟΙΗΣΗ ΜΕΣ ΣΤΗΝ ΠΟΙΗΣΗ

Bon dieu de bon dieu que j'ai envie
d'écrire un petit poème.
Tiens en voilà justement un qui passe
Petit petit petit.
                    RAYMOND QUENEAU

1

Αὐτές οἱ λέξεις σκάσανε σά ρόδι
Στά σκαλοπάτια τῶν καιρῶν πού ἔρχονται.
Σάν πυροτέχνημα ἔκρηξη θρύψαλα ἀστέρων
Ἤ — πιό σωστά — σάν ποίημα
Στόν οὐρανό τῆς μοναξιᾶς τῶν συνανθρώπων.

POETRY WITHIN POETRY

Bon dieu de bon dieu que j'ai envie
d'écrire un petit poème.
Tiens en voilà justement un qui passe
Petit petit petit.
                    RAYMOND QUENEAU

1

These words exploded like a pomegranate
On the doorstep of times to come.
Like a firework blast smithereens of stars
Or — more precisely — like a poem
In the sky of the solitude of our fellow men.

2

Σ' ἕνα ποίημα βρέχει ἀσταμάτητα
— *Comme il pleure dans mon cœur* —
Κι ἡ βροχή θά κρατάει γιά πάντα γιά πάντα
Σ' αὐτό τό βιβλίο θά βρίσκεται πάντα
Ἕνα φύλλο ὑγρό.

2

Inside a poem it rains incessantly
— *Comme il pleure dans mon coeur* —
And the rain will go on for ever and ever
In this book you will always find
A sodden leaf.

3

Στά ποιήματά μας σεργιανᾶνε πεθαμένοι
Οἱ στίχοι μας ἐγκυμονοῦνε τέρατα
Θά σηκωθοῦνε κάποτε ἀπό τάφους σά μῆτρες
Καί θά κουρνιάσουν τρέμοντας
Ἀπ' τό κρύο τοῦ αἰώνα.

3

In our poems dead men are wandering
Our lines are pregnant with monsters
One day they'll rise from womblike graves
And they'll perch trembling
From the chill of these times.

4

Πάνω στόν στίχο πού θά γράψω ἀκροβατῶ
Πάνω στόν στίχο πού 'χω γράψει ἰσορροπῶ·
Ἕνα κλαδί γερό εἶναι τό ποίημα
Πού δένω πότε πότε ἐκεῖ τήν κούνια μου
Νά αἰωροῦμαι πάνω ἀπό τό μαῦρο.

4

I walk the tightrope of the line I shall write
I am balanced on the line I have written;
The poem is a sturdy branch
From which I sometimes hang my swing
To hover over the blackness.

5

Ἐδῶ δέν βρίσκεται καθόλου ἕνα ποίημα
Σιντριβάνι ὀνείρου, ἐλιξήριον ἀγάπης —
Ἡ φιλοπαίγμων μου μονάχα φαντασία
Πού ἀκροβατεῖ ἀπό τή λέξη Ἐδῶ
Ὥς τήν τελεία μετά τή λέξη Καληνύχτα.

5

Here there is no poem at all
Fountain of dream, elixir of love —
Only my playful imagination
Walking the tightrope from the word Here
To the full stop after the word Goodnight.

6

Ποίημα τῶν πέντε μου στίχων καί τῶν πέντε μου αἰσθήσεων
Ποίημα πύργε Βαβέλ ἀνυψούμενε πύργε
Ἄς τρυπήσει ἀσυλλόγιστα ἡ ὀξεία σου μύτη
Τόν ψηλό οὐρανό — ἤ τήν πλούσια μήτρα —
Τῆς τυφλῆς μέχρι τρέλας αἰωνιότητας.

6

Poem of my five lines, my five senses,
Poem-Tower of Babel, tower erect,
Let your sharp spire unthinking penetrate
The lofty heavens — or the fertile womb —
Of eternity, almost crazy in its blindness.

7

Τώρα κοιμᾶσαι σ' ἁλμυρά χαλίκια
Σῶμα τῆς λύπης, στρῶμα τοῦ καιροῦ,
Πτῶμα ἐκβρασμένο ἀπ' τό κύμα τῆς μνήμης
Στήν ἀπόκρημνη ἀκτή
                      αὐτοῦ τοῦ ποιήματος.

7

Now you sleep on briny pebbles
Body of sorrow, bed of time,
Corpse washed up by memory's tide
On the rugged shore
                      of this poem.

8

Ποιήματά μου ἐσεῖς
Ποιό συρματόσκοινο μᾶς ἔχει ἑνώσει ἕως θανάτου
Ἐσεῖς, περικοκλάδες σ' ἕναν πύργο πού θά πέσει,
Ποιήματά μου σᾶς μισῶ
Μέ τό καταραμένο μίσος πού 'χουμε στόν ἑαυτό μας.

8

O you my poems
What metal wire has bound us together until death
You, bindweeds round a tower about to fall,
O you my poems I hate you
With this accursed hatred we keep for ourselves.

9

Αὐτό τό ποίημα
Εἶναι μιά χτισμένη σκάλα
— Ὅπως καί τ' ἄλλα βέβαια, μιά σκάλα —
Γιά ν' ἀνεβεῖτε ὥς τήν ψηλή της τήν κορφή
Νά δεῖτε, πίσω ἀπ' τις γραμμές, τή νύχτα πού ἀνατέλλει.

9

This poem
Is built like a staircase
Like all the rest, a staircase
For you to climb to the very top
To see, behind its lines, the night rising.

10
Ἐδῶ ἤτανε κάποτε ἕνα ποίημα
Ἐμπόδιο τοῦ καιροῦ, φτερό τῶν πόθων.
Ἐρείπιο κατάντησε
Μιά μαύρη τρύπα κι ἄσκημη κατάντησε
Τέσσερις πέντε στίχοι πού καπνίζουν.

10

Here there used to be a poem
Holding back time, token of desires.
It ended up in ruins
It ended up a black and filthy hollow
Four or five lines, smouldering.

11
Αὐτό τό ποίημα γράφει αὐτό τό ποίημα
Κόβει ἀπ' τό σῶμα του καί τρέφει τόν ἑαυτό του.
Οἱ λέξεις του τινάζονται ψηλά καί ξαναπέφτουνε
Ἀνοίγει δρόμο μές στό χιόνι τῆς σελίδας —
Ἔκπληκτος βλέπω νά μοῦ ἀποκαλύπτεται.

11

This poem writes this poem
It cuts bits off its body to feed itself.
Its words shoot in the air high and fall back down
It drives a road through the snow of the page —
Astonished I watch as it reveals itself to me.

12

Μ' αὐτό τό ποίημα παίζουμε ἀπόψε
Σᾶς τό πετάω καί τό πετᾶτε πίσω
Τ' ἀνοίγουμε στά δυό κι οἱ λέξεις χύνονται.

Γιατί ἄν νωρίς δέν σ' ἐξουδετερώσουμε
— Ἄτιμο ποίημα — θά μᾶς γονατίσεις.

12

Tonight we're playing with this poem
I throw it to you and you throw it back to me
We split it in two and the words gush out.

For if we don't do away with you in time
— You bastard poem — you'll bring us to our knees.

13
Τή νύχτα ἔβλεπε στόν ὕπνο του ἕνα στίχο
Πού νά ψηλώνει ἀτέλειωτα.
Τρυπώντας τό οὐράνιο περίβλημα
Ἀρχίζανε νά πέφτουν
                    τά ὑπερκόσμια σκεύη.

13

At night he dreamed of a line of verse
Growing taller and taller.
Piercing the celestial envelope
Utensils from on high
                        began tumbling down.

14
Ἕνα σύννεφο ποίημα
                    αἰωρεῖται στόν ἀέρα.
Ἐλᾶτε νά χορέψουμε γυμνοί —
Μήπως βρέξει
            σ' αὐτή τή σελίδα.

14
A cloud poem
             is suspended in the air.
Let us dance naked —
Hoping it may rain
             on this page.

15
Ἡ νύχτα ἀπόψε βρέχει ὅλους τοὺς φόβους μου.
Εἰς σὲ προστρέχω τέχνη τῆς ποιήσεως
Χτίζω μὲ νύχια καὶ μὲ δόντια ἕνα ποίημα
Λαχανιασμένος μπαίνω νὰ προφυλαχτῶ
Καὶ κλείνω πίσω μου τὸν τελευταῖο στίχο.

15
This night is raining all my fears.
To thee I turn O art of poetry
With nails and teeth I build a poem
Gasping for breath I enter its shelter
And slam the last line shut behind me.

ΠΟΙΗΣΗ ΜΕΣ ΣΤΗΝ ΠΟΙΗΣΗ

16
Τό ποίημα.
Μοτοσικλέτες
Καί μηχανοκίνητα
Στό ἄσπρο
Τοπίο.

16
The poem.
Motorbikes
And tanks
In the white
Landscape.

Ο ΑΣΩΤΟΣ

Θά ἐξαργυρώσω μέ λέξεις ἐπίχρυσες
Τίς ράβδους σκοταδιοῦ πού σταθερά ἀποθήκευα
Στά θησαυροφυλάκια τοῦ στήθους.

Θά πάρω ἔπειτα τούς δρόμους
Μ' ἑκατομμύρια ποιήματα
Σκορπίζοντας στούς τίμιους συμπολίτες μου
Τήν ἀναπάντεχη κληρονομιά
Τῆς φτώχειας.

THE PRODIGAL

I'll cash in gilded words
Ingots of darkness I've been saving
In the treasury of my breast.

Then I'll take to the streets
With millions of poems
Dishing out to my fellow citizens
The unexpected legacy
Of destitution.

ΑΝΕΠΙΔΕΚΤΟΙ ΑΘΑΝΑΣΙΑΣ

Τρεῖς ὧρες φτάνουν γιά νά γράψεις ἕνα ὡραῖο ποίημα
Ὅμως τριάντα χρόνια δέν ἀρκοῦν νά γράψεις ἕνα ποίημα
Ὅσο ἄν ζητᾶς κι ἄν θυσιάζεις. Ἡ ἄνοιξη
Κατάλαβα πώς εἶναι ὑπόθεση ρουτίνας γιά τή φύση
Πού ἐχθρεύεται τό πνεῦμα καί ἀμαυρώνει τό ἄφθαρτο.
Σκέψου καλά: Κάθε μορφή ἀθανασίας ἀντίκειται
Στήν ἔννοια τοῦ ὄντος. Κάθε ἀντίθεση
Θά συντριβεῖ κάτω ἀπ' τή φτέρνα τοῦ καιροῦ
Καθώς πατάει μέ δρασκελιές καί πέλματα γρανίτη. Ἀνοίγοντας
Μιά ὑπόνοια παρόντος
Καίγοντας
Τά φρύγανα τῶν πράξεων σέ οὐρανομήκεις φλόγες ἥλιου.
Ὅπου παρόν
Σημαίνει ἁπλῶς τό παρελθόν τοῦ μέλλοντος
Ἤ, πιό σωστά, τό μέλλον ἑνός ἄλλου παρελθόντος
Ἀφοῦ, ὅσο ξέρω, δέν ὑπάρχει ἀκόμα ἡ συνταγή
Νά φτιαχτεῖ μιά στιγμή διαρκείας. Τί ἄπληστοι
Σταθήκαμε στ' ἀλήθεια τί ἄσωτοι
Μές στή φιλαργυρία μας. Ποιός θά πιστέψει ἄραγε
Πώς σπαταλήσαμε τή λίγη αἰωνιότητα πού μᾶς ἀναλογεῖ
Χαμένοι σέ μιάν ἔρημο ἀπό λέξεις. Σπέρνοντας
Καί περιμένοντας τό νέο φροῦτο πού θά βγεῖ ἀπ' τό κουκούτσι,
    ἀφήνοντας
Τό γινωμένο φροῦτο νά σαπίσει.
                      Ἀλήθεια, τί ἄπραγοι
Τί ἀνεπίδεκτοι ἀθανασίας οἱ θνητοί.

IMPERVIOUS TO IMMORTALITY

Three hours are enough to write a nice poem
But thirty years are not sufficient to write a poem
No matter how much you seek or sacrifice. Spring
I reckon is a routine matter for nature
Which detests the spirit and sullies the imperishable.
Think carefully: Every form of immortality is opposed
To the notion of being. Every opposition
Will be crushed by the heel of time
As it strides on granite soles. Introducing
A hint of the present
Burning
The kindling of deeds in a sky-high solar blaze.
Where the present
Means simply the past of the future
Or, more precisely, the future of another past
Since, as I know, the formula doesn't yet exist
To concoct a lasting moment. How greedy
We've been indeed how prodigal
Amidst our parsimony. For who would believe
That we've spent the bit of eternity allotted to us
Lost in a desert of words. Sowing
And waiting for the new fruit that will spring from the seed,
    leaving
The ripe fruit to rot.
                  Indeed, how untouched by
How impervious to immortality we mortals are.

ΟΤΙ ΤΟΝ ΠΟΙΗΤΗΝ ΔΕΟΙ
ΕΙΠΕΡ ΜΕΛΛΟΙ ΠΟΙΗΤΗΣ ΕΙΝΑΙ

Ὁ παφλασμός γεννάει τή θάλασσα κι ἰδού ἡ φωνή
Βγάζει λαρύγγι πού ὁμιλεῖ. Ἀλίμονο·
Ὁ μαραγκός χωρίς τά ξύλα του δέν μοιάζει μαραγκός
Ἀνελλιπῶς ζητάει τόν ἦχο τοῦ σφυριοῦ νά μαρτυράει
Τήν τέχνη του.
                      Γι' αὐτό σοῦ λέω
Πάρε χαρτί πιάσε μολύβι κι ἄρχισε —
Τόν πρῶτο στίχο, ἄν δέν στόν δώσουν οἱ θεοί, δανείσου τον:

Ὁ παφλασμός γεννάει τή θάλασσα κι ἰδού ἡ φωνή

THAT THE POET MUST
IF HE WOULD BE A POET

The splash of surf generates the sea and behold the voice
Creates a larynx which speaks. Alas;
The carpenter is no carpenter without his wood
He needs the constant sound of the hammer to bear witness
To his art.
        That's why I tell you:
Grab a pen, get paper and begin —
If the gods don't grant you the first line, borrow it:

The splash of surf generates the sea and behold the voice

Ο ΗΧΟΣ ΤΩΝ ΛΕΞΕΩΝ

Οἱ λέξεις μου εἶναι ξύλινες. Τίς βάφω μαῦρες, τίς κρεμάω μέ προσοχή ἀπ' τό ταβάνι. Ὁ ἀέρας τῶν ἡμερῶν περνάει ἀπ' τά παράθυρα, κουνώντας τις ἀδέξια. Ἔξω καί μέσα στό δωμάτιο εἶναι νύχτα, ἀκούω μόνο τό νωθρό τους θρόισμα καθώς στριφογυρνᾶνε. Καμιά φορά χτυπιοῦνται μεταξύ τους, καί τότε βγαίνουν ἦχοι ἀναπάντεχοι: καμπάνα σέ κωμόπολη πού ἁπλώνεται φωτιά — ρόγχος ἀρρώστου πού τοῦ τρώει ὁ χρόνος τό λαρύγγι — βιολί ἀπό τά νύχια ἑνός πουλιοῦ — ἔκρηξη σ' ἐργοστάσιο μέ τέσσερις νεκρούς κι ἑξήντα τραυματίες — πιστόλι νά ἐκλιπαρεῖ — γέλιο νά κλαίει.

THE SOUND OF WORDS

My words are made of wood. I paint them black, hang them carefully from the ceiling. The wind of the days comes in through the windows shaking them roughly. Outside and inside the room it's night, I hear only their idle rustle as they revolve. Sometimes they crash together, and unexpected sounds are produced: a bell in a small town where fire is spreading — a groan of an ailing man, his throat being devoured by time — a violin plucked by the claws of a bird — a blast in a factory, four dead and sixty wounded — a pistol that begs for mercy — laughter sobbing.

Ο ΗΧΟΣ ΤΟΥ ΚΟΣΜΟΥ

Μικρή μου γόησσα μήν ἀποκρούεις τόν ἔρωτά μου —
Πάντως νά ξέρεις πώς δέ σ' ἔχω ἐρωτευτεῖ.
Κι ἄν σέ τραγούδησαν
Οἱ ποιητές τῶν ἐποχῶν κι ἄν σοῦ 'ψαλαν
Μέ λύρες ἀπό τρίχινες χορδές
Μάθε λοιπόν, οἱ ποιητές εἶναι μαλάκες ὅλοι τους
Ἀλλιῶς δέν θ' ἄφηναν
Νά τούς φωνάζουν ποιητές. Ἀκούμπησε
Τό τρυφερό χεράκι σου ἀπό νερό κι ἀπό ἄνεμο
— Ἔτσι δέ μίλαγαν αὐτοί οἱ ἀνεκδιήγητοι; —
Στό μέτωπό μου. Ὁ πυρετός
Ἡ φυσική θερμοκρασία ἑνός κορμιοῦ
Πού κατουράει τή δάφνη καί ἀψηφάει τόν ψίθυρο
Τοῦ πνεύματος πού ξεψυχάει. Ἀκούμπησε
Τή ρόγα τοῦ βυζιοῦ στά χείλια μου
Κι ἄσε τή γλώσσα μου νά γλείψει ἄλαλη
Τό βάζο τοῦ ρίγους σου. Γόησσα μικρή
Μέ στίχους δέν ὑψώνεται κανείς σέ ὀργασμό
Οὔτε τά ψώνια ἐτοῦτα γύρω σου πού χύνουνε
Γαργάρες ἀπό λέξεις. Ἄκουσε
Τούς παφλασμούς τά μουγκρητά ἤ τά κλάματα:
Μέ τέτοιους ἤχους πλάστηκε ὁ κόσμος. Ἄκουσε
Τό κρώξιμο — ἤ τόν βρυχηθμό
Τοῦ λιονταριοῦ πού εἶναι ὁ κόσμος. Ἄκουσε
Τό βουητό τοῦ ὠκεανοῦ. Τό βουητό·
Κι ὄχι τό ἀμέριμνο τραγούδι τῶν ψαράδων.

THE SOUND OF THE WORLD

My little enchantress do not fend off my love —
In any case you should know I'm not in love with you.
And if the poets of the ages sang to you
And if they chanted for you
To lyres with strings of hair,
Then you should know, the poets are all jerks
Otherwise they wouldn't let
Themselves be called poets. Rest
Your delicate hand made of water and wind
— Isn't that how they spoke those idiots? —
On my forehead. Fever
The body's natural temperature
That pisses on the laurels and cares nothing for the whisper
Of the expiring spirit. Rest
The nipple of your breast against my lips
And let my tongue caress unspeaking
The place of your excitement. Little enchantress
No one reaches orgasm through verse
Not even these screwballs around you ejaculating
Word-gargles. Listen
To the splashes, the moans or the cries:
With such sounds the world was created. Listen
To the screech — or the roaring
Of the lion that the world is. Listen
To the clamour of the ocean's drone. The clamour;
Not the fishermen's carefree lyric.

ΓΕΝΕΣΗ

Ὅσο προχώραγα στό φῶς
Τά χρώματα ὠχραίνανε
Πυκνῶναν στροβιλίζονταν σά δίσκος
Γίνονταν
Τό χρῶμα αὐτό πού χρῶμα πιά
δέν ἦταν.

Βαθιά στή νύχτα οἱ δρόμοι διακλαδίζονται
Ἀνοίγονται σέ νέους συνδυασμούς
Εἶπα «σκοτάδι» καί ἰδού ἐγένετο
Ἡ γῆ μέ τά φυτά της μέ τά ζῶα της
Ἀόρατα πελώρια τρυφερά
Καί νά μοῦ μοιάζουν.

GENESIS

As I marched into the light
Colours were losing their colour
Condensing, whirling like disks
Becoming
This colour which is a colour
No more.

In the depth of night roads split apart
Open to new conjunctions
I said "darkness" and behold there
Was the earth with its plants its animals
Invisible immense and delicate
And in my likeness.

Η ΣΚΕΨΗ ΑΝΗΚΕΙ ΣΤΟ ΠΕΝΘΟΣ

Ἐγκαταλείπω ξανά τή σιωπή τῆς ψυχῆς μου
Καί μπαινοβγαίνω στά ἐκκωφαντικά λιθογραφεῖα
Τοῦ τίποτα. (Πέτρινοι κύλινδροι ἀλέθουν συλλαβές
Νά μή μᾶς λείψει τό ἐπιούσιο ποίημα). Μαῦρο ψωμί
Μέ μαῦρο ἀλεύρι — ἀναρωτήθηκε ἄραγε κανείς
Γιατί στό τύπωμα βγαίνουν οἱ λέξεις
Μαῦρες;
Ποιά γενετήσια κλίση ἀποφάσισε
Πώς εἶναι πένθος κάθε σκέψη; Ποιό ἔνστικτο
Ρίχνει χαστούκι στά εὔοσμα
Παιδιά τῆς σημειολογίας
Πού ἄφησαν
Σκανδαλωδῶς νά τούς ξεφύγει τό ἐμφανές;

(Προσποιούμενος συχνά συγκινήσεις
Κατάντησα εὐαίσθητος.

Καί μέ τί χέρια νά ζυμώσεις τώρα τό ψωμί
Μέ τί κουράγιο νά τελειώσεις ποίημα).

THOUGHT BELONGS
TO MOURNING

Again I abandon the silence of my soul
I come and go among the ear-splitting printshops
Of nothing. (Stone cylinders grind syllables
So we're not deprived of the daily poem.) Black bread
With black flour — did anybody ever wonder
Why in print words turn out
Black?
What sexual leaning decided
That every thought is in mourning? What instinct
Strikes the sweet-smelling
Children of Semiotics
Who, scandalously,
Let the obvious escape?

(Feigning emotions again and again
In the end I became sensitive.

And with what hands now would you knead the bread
With what courage would you end a poem.)

ΠΟΤΑΜΙ ΠΟΙΗΜΑ

Ἔπεσα σέ λάκκο μέ ἄσπρο καί κάηκα.

Ὅμως τό ποίημα εἶναι ποτάμι
Καί μιά ὑγρασία θαυμαστική
Θαρρῶ γλυκαίνει τή σιωπή ἀπ' τήν ὀργή της
Ἄν τήν πρόδωσα. Δέ φταίω, τ' ὁρκίζομαι.
Κάποιοι ξεχάσαν ἕνα βάζο μέ φωνήεντα στό ράφι
Ποῦ θά τό 'φτανα. Ὕστερα ἔμαθα μέ φλοῦδες συλλαβῶν
Νά φτιάνω πλοῖα. Μικρά, ὅσο τό δάχτυλο παιδιοῦ
Καί τά 'ριχνα μές στό νεράκι πού ἔφευγε —
Τότε κατάλαβα: Μονάχα ὁ χωρισμός
ἑνώνει τούς ἀνθρώπους. Τά ὑπόλοιπα
Τά ξέρετε ἀπό ἄλλες διηγήσεις. Πῶς «πίσω δέν γυρνάει»
Πῶς «δίς ἐμβῆναι τῷ αὐτῷ οὐκ ἔστιν» καί τά ὅμοια.
Μᾶς τά 'παν, τά ξανάπαν, σάν τό αὐτονόητο
Νά εἶχε χρείαν ἑρμηνείας. Ἀλλά τό ποίημα
Εἶναι ποτάμι ἀπό δάκρυα ξένα. Παιδί πού ἀντρώθηκε
Συχνά τό βλέπω νά γυρνάει πρός τήν πηγούλα του.
Κι ὅταν φουσκώνει
Ἀπ' τήν πολλήν ἀγάπη,

    Πνίγει.

RIVER POEM

I fell into pit of whiteness and got burned.

But the poem is a river
And a flattering moistness
I guess it sweetens the wrath of its silence
Should I ever betray it. I swear, it's not my fault.
A vase of vowels was left on the shelf
That I would reach for. Later I learned to make boats
With skins of syllables. Small, as a child's finger
And used to toss them into the water flowing past —
Then I understood: only separation
unites people. You know the rest
From other tales. That "it never turns back"
That "one cannot step into the same one twice" and the like.
They told us, and told us again, as if the self-evident
Needed explication. But the poem
Is a river of foreign tears. A child grown into a man
I often see it turning back to its source.
And when it swells
From too much love,

    It chokes.

ΕΝΩΠΙΟΝ ΑΚΡΟΑΤΗΡΙΟΥ

Πήγαινα νύχτα παρά θῖν' ἁλός
Κι ἀπάγγελλα ἀπό μέσα μου καινούργιους στίχους.
Θύελλα στό ἀκροατήριο
Μέ ἠχηρά χειροκροτήματα πού φτάναν κατά κύματα
Ἐπευφημίες καί γιούχα τῶν ἀφρῶν.
Αὐτό στ' ἀλήθεια εἶναι κοινό!
Μέ τό ρευστό τῶν λέξεων στά κόκαλά του,
Ἀμφίθυμο
Ἀπ' τήν ἀστάθεια τῶν σημαινομένων. Ἡ ἔμπνευση
Ρυτίδωνε τό δέρμα του ὅλο ρίγη
Κι ἦταν βυθός ἡ ἐπιφάνεια πού ἀλάλαζε
Στά σκοτεινά.

Ποιός ἄλλος πίστεψε ποτέ ὅτι τά ποιήματα
Εἶναι ὁ βόγκος τοῦ νεροῦ
Πού σπάει καί ντρέπεται
Ζητώντας μόνο νά χαθεῖ σ' ἕν' ἄλλο βόγκο;

Ἄς εἴμαστε λιγότερο μικρόψυχοι. Ἕρπει ἡ φειδώ
Μέ κρύο αἷμα δαψιλεύεται
Μικρά ψιχία. Ὅμως τά ποιήματα
Δέν ἐπαιτοῦν τόν ἔπαινο
Οὔτε τή στάλα τό μελάνι ἀπό τόν κάλαμο
Τοῦ κάθε κριτικοῦ. Διψοῦν μιά θύελλα βρυχηθμῶν
Μιά λαοθάλασσα
Νά τρέμει σύγκορμη ἀπ' τή ρώμη τῶν ρημάτων
Ἤ νά σφυρίζει ἔστω
Μιά γελοία παρήχηση (σάν τήν πιό πάνω)
Ἀφρίζοντας
Ἀπό ἔκσταση κι ἀπό θυμό.

Μή σᾶς γελᾶ ἡ σεμνότητα
Καί τά sub specie aeternitatis
Τῶν μιξοπάρθενων. Ὅλοι φοβοῦνται

BEFORE AN AUDIENCE

I was walking along by the sea at night
And reciting to myself new lines of verse.
A storm in the auditorium
With roaring applause coming in waves
Cheers and catcalls from the surf.
That indeed is an audience!
With words flowing in its bones,
Wavering
With the instability of the signified. Inspiration
Was rippling its skin into wrinkles
And the seabed and the bellowing surface
In the darkness were one.

Who else ever believed that poems
Are the groaning of water
That breaks and withdraws
Seeking only to lose itself in another groan?

Let us be less miserly. Thrift slithers
In cold blood disbursing
Small scraps. But poems
Beg neither for praise
Nor for a drop of ink from a critic's
Quill. They thirst for a roaring tempest
A sea of people
Bodies vibrating with the violence of the verbs
Or even whistling at
Some silly alliteration (like the above)
Foaming
In ecstasy and anger.

Do not be fooled by the modesty
And the *sub specie aeternitatis*
Of the would-be virgins. All afraid of

Ὅλοι ποθοῦνε ἀχόρταγα
Τό ἐφήμερο.

Ἐπευφημίες καί γιούχα.

BEFORE AN AUDIENCE

All longing insatiably for
The ephemeral.

Cheers and catcalls.

ΜΕΤΑΠΟΙΗΣΗ

Πνέει ἀέρας φωνηέντων. Ἀέναη
Ἀκινησία τῶν νοημάτων καί ὁλάνθιστες
Περικοκλάδες λόγου. Τί ὄμορφα
Πού γουργουρίζουν μές στή θαλπωρή τοῦ παλαιοῦ
Οἱ καινοτόμοι. Τί ἔνταση
Στά ἐργαστήρια τῶν μεταποιητῶν.
(Ὁ Ρίλκε δέν σηκώνει πλέον μετασκευή. Γιά πέταμα.
Ὅμως τοῦ Πάουντ, λέει, στενεύουνε τά πέτα
Καί στό μπλουτζίν τοῦ Γκίνσμπεργκ ταίριαξε σακάκι τουήντ
Ἀντί γιά τζάκετ). Τί ἄραγε
Νά εἶναι αὐτό πού δέν ὑπῆρχε πρίν, καί τώρα ὑπάρχει;
Μήν ἀπαντᾶτε πρόχειρα. Ἀφοῦ ἀπάντησε πρίν χρόνια ὁ
Ἐμπεδοκλῆς, μήν ἀπαντᾶτε. Γίγνεσθαι πάρος οὐκ ἐόν
Πῶς θά 'ταν δυνατόν; Κι ἄν θέτε ἀλλιῶς:
Τ' ἐόν ἐξαπολέσθαι ἀνήνυστον — ποῦ ἀκούστηκε
Νά πέθανε κανένας ζωντανός; Ἀμέριμνος
Γυρίζει ἐντούτοις ὁ τροχός τῶν ἐποχῶν
Καί ἀνθίζουνε
Τά στόματα τῶν νέων. Πού χύνουνε
Ἀβέρτα τό παλιό κρασί
Σέ ἀσκιά καινούργια. Ἐπιμελῶς μπλαζέ
Μπαλαμουτιάζονται μέσα στό δρόμο, ἐλπίζοντας
Νά σκανδαλίσουν λίγο τούς ἀστούς. Ἤ μ' ἀλυσίδες
Καί καρφιά στά πέτσινα
Καταπτοοῦν τά τρομαλέα γεροντάκια. Βρέ ἀνίδεοι
Ποιός ἀπό σᾶς μπορεῖ νά γίνει πάλι Ἀλκιβιάδης
Πού, ἀφοῦ ξεσκίστηκε ὅλη νύχτα μ' ἕνα λόχο, ἐκεῖ στό χάραμα
Ὅρμησε κι ἔκοψε τ' ἀρχίδια ἀπ' τίς Ἑρμές, ἀφήνοντας
Εὐνοῦχο ἕνα θεό; Ἀναρχικούληδες
Τῶν βόρειων προαστίων καί τοῦ κέντρου, ποιός νά ὑπέθετε
Πώς τέτοια ὑπέρλαμπρα ὑποδείγματα προγόνων θά 'βγαζαν
Τόσο ξενέρωτα φρικιά!
Δέν ξέρω. Ἀξύνετοι ἀκούσαντες
Κωφοῖσιν ἐοίκασιν. Ἀλλά ἐσεῖς βεβαίως ποῦ ν' ἀκούσετε

METAPOETRY

A wind of vowels is blowing. Eternal
Immobility of meanings and discourse
Periwinkles all abloom. How prettily
The innovators coo inside the comfort
Of the old. What intensity
In the workrooms of the metapoets.
(Rilke supports no more refashioning. For the bin.
But Pound's lapels, it's said, should be narrowed
And Ginsberg's jeans needed a tweed coat
Instead of denim). What is this, I wonder,
Which did not exist before, and now exists?
Don't answer off-hand. Empedocles answered
Years ago, so don't answer. *Can that come into being
which existed not before?* How could that be so? Or if you wish:
Impossible for that to perish which existed hitherto.
Whoever heard of someone dying alive? Careless
Nonetheless turns the seasons' wheel
And flourish now
The mouths of the young. Who pour
Without heed the old wine
Into new skins. Affectedly blasé
Making out in public, hoping
To scandalize the bourgeois a bit. Or with chains
And spikes on leatherwear
Intimidate the timid oldies. You morons
Which one of you can be Alcibiades again
Who, after fucking all night long a whole platoon,
Dashed around at dawn cutting the balls
Off all the herms, making a eunuch of a god?
You petty, uptown-downtown anarchists, who could suppose
That such shining examples of ancestors could give way
To such freaky nerds!
I don't know. *Fools though they hear
Be like unto the deaf.* But you, how can you hear at all

ΜΕΤΑΠΟΙΗΣΗ

Μέ τά γουόκμαν διαπασῶν. Σᾶς τρόμαξαν
Καί τά τσιγάρτοι τσιγαροῦν — σά νά χρειάζεται
Πιό λίγος κόπος νά ξεμάθεις τό γνωστό. Μά διάολε
Λιγάκι ἄν ξύνατε δυό τρία τσιγαροῦν θά βρίσκατε
Τουλάχιστον μπαρούτι. Ὄχι νά κάθεστε
Τέλη εἰκοστοῦ
Νά μαλακίζεστε ἀκόμα
       μέ μολότοφ.

With headphones at full volume. Intimidated
By those *therefores* and *therefore-indeeds* — as if it takes
Less labour to unlearn what's known. But damn it,
If you'd just scraped one or two *therefore-indeeds*
You'd have at least found gunpowder. Not be sitting here
End of the twentieth century
Still jerking off
                with molotov cocktails.

Η ΠΟΙΗΣΗ ΔΕΝ ΓΙΝΕΤΑΙ ΜΕ ΙΔΕΕΣ

Πνεῦμα σημαίνει φύσημα.

Ὅμως μή σπεύδεις. Ἄλλο τό ἕωλο
Ρουθούνισμα μιᾶς αὔρας ἄλλο ἡ λαίλαπα
Ἑνός γεροῦ βοριᾶ. Καί πῶς ἐσύ
Μέ πρωτοβάθμια σκέψη νά ἐκπορθήσεις
Ποίημα;
Θυμᾶσαι: «Πρέπει πρῶτα νά συλλάβει ὁ νοῦς
Κι ἔπειτα ἡ καρδιά θερμά νά αἰσθανθεῖ».
Σαφεῖς οἱ ὁδηγίες. Λακωνικότατες.
Καί ὅταν λέμε «πρῶτα νά συλλάβει ὁ νοῦς»
Δέν ἐννοοῦμε σίγουρα τόπους κοινούς. Ἀθέατα
Νυστέρια ὁλόγυρα ὀρθοτομοῦν τά βάθη
Ἐγκέφαλοι μιᾶς νέας ἐποχῆς ἐκφράζουνε
Τό ἀόριστο
Μέ ὅλως ἀκριβῆ
Ἀοριστία.

Ὅπως καί νά 'χει
Ὁ Μαλλαρμέ τό ἀπέκλεισε:
«Ἡ ποίηση δέν γίνεται μέ ἰδέες»
(Ὡραία ἰδέα. Μπορεῖ νά γίνει ποίημα;
Δύσκολο).

Ἄρα
Σοῦ μένει τό αἴσθημα.

Τό αἴσθημα σοῦ μένει
Συντριβῆς
Γιά τόν αἰώνιο θρίαμβο

Τῶν αἰσθημάτων.

POETRY IS NOT MADE
WITH IDEAS

Spirit just means breathing.

But not so fast. The sniffle
Of a stale breeze is one thing but
A strong northern gust is another. How can you
Take possession of a poem
With elementary thinking?
Remember: "The intellect must first conceive
And then the heart should feel with passion."
Clear instructions. Most laconic.
And when we say: "the intellect must first conceive"
Surely we don't mean common tropes. All around
Invisible scalpels cut down into the depths
Masterminds of a new age express
The indefinite
With utterly precise
Indefinition.

No matter what
Mallarmé excluded it:
"Poetry is not made with ideas"
(Nice idea. Can it make a poem?
Difficult).

Then
You are left with feeling.

The feeling you are left with
Of devastation
At the eternal triumph

Of feelings.

ΚΑΘΑΡΣΗ

Ἕνας νεφρός μέσα σέ ποίημα
Ξενίζει.
Σάν ψεύτικος νά φαίνεται, σάν τεχνητός.
Ὅμως ἄν ἄνοιξα τέτοια κουβέντα, εἶναι πού ἤθελα
Νά σᾶς ρωτήσω: Τί ἄραγε
Μοιάζει κοντύτερα σ' ἕνα νεφρό;
Τό πάγκρεας; Τό νέφος; Ὁ ἀφρός;

Καγχάζουν γύρω οἱ ἀγχίνοες
Γιά τήν ἀφέλεια τῆς ἀπορίας. Δέν ξέρουνε
Πώς ὅ,τι συγγενεύει ἐδῶ, ἐκ τοῦ σύνεγγυς,
Μόνον ἐδῶ, ἐκ τοῦ σύνεγγυς, θά συγγενεύει.
Ἀκοῦστε με. Γιά βγεῖτε παραέξω ἐξαργυρώσετε
Καρδιές — βραδιές
Χέρια — μαχαίρια
Ἡ τοῦ ἀέρα
Τίς ἀόρατες ἀορτές. Καμιά πραγματικότητα
Δέν πρόκειται νά στέρξει
Τέτοια παραχάραξη.
Καμιά παρήχηση
Δέν ἀπηχεῖ τά γεγονότα.

Ἕνας νεφρός στό ποίημα
Ξενίζει.
Δύο νεφροί στό σῶμα
Εἶναι ἀγλάισμα. Ἰδού
Ἐνώπιόν σας ἡ θανάσιμη ἀντίφαση
Τό ἐξόφθαλμο σκάνδαλο.

Μά ποῦ νά βρεῖς
Τόν σθεναρό εἰσαγγελέα
Νά τολμήσει
Κάθαρση.

PURGATION

A kidney inside a poem
Strikes you as wrong.
Seems fake, an artificial one.
But if I've started to talk like this, it is because
I'd like to ask you: which do you think
Is most like a kidney?
The pancreas? The kid? Or Sidney?

All around the savvy sneer
At the naive question. They do not know
That what is close here, by close reading,
Only here, in close reading, will be close.
Listen to me. Why don't you try exchanging
Hearts — darts
Lives — knives
Or the air's
Invisible veins. No actuality
Will actually endorse
Such a forgery.
No alliteration
Reiterates the facts.

A kidney in a poem
Strikes you as wrong.
Two kidneys in the body
Pride and glory. Behold
In front of you the lethal contradiction
The eye-bulging scandal.

But where will you find
The Public Prosecutor
Tough enough to brave
Purgation.

ΑΠΟ ΤΟ ΠΟΙΗΜΑ ΒΓΑΙΝΕΙΣ ΠΑΝΤΑ ΖΩΝΤΑΝΟΣ

Ἕνας νεκρός μέσα στό ποίημα
Δέν ξενίζει. Ἀντίθετα.
Κρανία μέλη ὡραῖα κορμιά
Διάσπαρτα
Σέ λέξεις φόβου
Σέ φορμόλη νοσταλγίας
Ἀκέραια
Πτώματα ἐξαίσια
Τῶν αἰσθημάτων.
Καί αὐτόχειρες
Ἰδανικοί βεβαίως (γνωρίζετε
τή σημασία ἐδῶ τοῦ «ἰδανικοί»)
Ὅποια σελίδα νά σηκώσεις.

Καλότυχοι νεκροί αὐτοί,
Πού λησμονᾶμε
Πόσο ἀνύπαρκτοι στ᾽ ἀλήθεια ὑπήρξανε.

Ὅταν ἀλλοῦ
(Πάλι γνωρίζετε τί λέμε «ἀλλοῦ»)
Τό αἷμα χύνεται
Τό αἷμα κρυώνει
Τό αἷμα θρομβώνεται
(Ἀδυνατεῖ νά κάνει ὡραίους στίχους
ἡ πραγματικότης, βλέπετε)
Κι οἱ μεταστάσεις θριαμβεύουν
Μέ ἅλματα
Εἰς βάθος.

Δέν εἶναι ὁ τομογράφος στυλογράφος
(Οἱ εὔκολες
μεταφορές πονᾶνε τέτοιες ὧρες)
Οὔτε ἡ νάρκωση τοῦ χειρουργείου δοκιμάζεται

YOU ALWAYS EMERGE ALIVE FROM A POEM

A dead body inside a poem
Doesn't strike you as wrong. On the contrary.
Skulls limbs beautiful torsos
Scattered
In words of dread
In the formaldehyde of nostalgia
Intact
Exquisite corpses
Of sensations.
And suicides
Ideal certainly (you get the meaning
of "ideal" here)
No matter which page you turn.

Fortunate those *dead*
That we don't recall
How unreal they really were.

When elsewhere
(Again you get why we say "elsewhere")
Blood is spilled
Blood freezes
Blood forms clots
(Reality, you see,
cannot make beautiful lines)
And metastases triumph
With high-jumps
Into the depths.

Tomography is not calligraphy
(Easy metaphors
are painful at such moments)
And you can't try medical sedation

ΑΠΟ ΤΟ ΠΟΙΗΜΑ ΒΓΑΙΝΕΙΣ ΠΑΝΤΑ ΖΩΝΤΑΝΟΣ

Πάνω σέ ἄλγη
Ἐν φαντασίᾳ
Καί λόγῳ.

Ἄς μή γελιόμαστε.

Ἀπό τό ποίημα βγαίνεις πάντα ζωντανός.

On ailments
That lie in fantasy
And words.

Let's just not kid ourselves.

You always emerge alive from a poem.

ΤΑ ΛΟΓΙΑ ΜΕΝΟΥΝ

Χτές διάβασα ξανά τά ποιήματά μου
Κι ἔμεινα
Πραγματικά ἐνεός. Κυρίως μέ κλόνισε
Ἡ πλησμονή τοῦ ἔρωτα —
Πού ἀπουσιάζει ὁλότελα.
Ἐγώ εἶμ' αὐτός;
Πού ἄν μέ ρωτοῦσαν, θά 'λεγα
Πῶς θά 'πρεπε λιγότερο προσωπικά
Νά 'χα μιλήσει. Ποιά αἰσχυντηλή
Λογοκρισία χωρίς ντροπή ἀποφάσιζε
Μ' ἄλλα φορέματα κάθε φορά
Νά ντύνει τά γεγυμνωμένα καί ἄλλαζε
Τόν ροῦν στήν κοίτη; Ἔμεινα

Πραγματικά ἐνεός.

Δέν ξέρω τί θ' ἀποφανθοῦν (ἄν, ὅποτε)
Οἱ αὐθέντες οἱ αὐθεντικοί ἐτάζοντες
Καρδίες καί ὄργανα λοιπά·
Ἴσως προσάψουν ἐρεβώδη σαρκασμό
Τή μεταμφίεση τοῦ ἐλεγείου σέ σάτιρα
Τή λέξη πού διστάζει ἀμφίσημη
Σέ σκοινί τρόμου —
Ἀνάρμοστο
Νά ὑποθέσω ἐδῶ τί ἐνδέχεται
Νά ὑποθέσουν ἄλλοι.

Τό μόνο πού μέ ἀνησυχεῖ
(Καθόλου δέ μέ ἀνησυχεῖ, ἀστειεύομαι)
Εἶναι πού ἀπ' ὅσα ἔγραψα
Ἀπό ἐκεῖ μονάχα θά μέ νιώσουν.
Στίχος γνωστός, καβαφικός. Καί ἀξίωμα.
Μά περισσότερο ἀντικλείδι γιά ν' ἀνοίγουνε
Τά πιό ἀνοιχτά συρτάρια ἐξιχνιάζοντας
Φέρνοντας ἄνετα στό φῶς οἱ κρίνοντες
Τά φανερά. Συνθῆκες βίου προσωπικοῦ,

THE SPOKEN WORDS REMAIN

Yesterday I read my poems again
And I was rendered
Practically speechless. Mainly I was shocked by
The abundance of love —
Which is totally absent.
Is that me?
If people asked, I'd say
That I should have spoken
Less personally. What bashful
Censorship shamelessly decided
To cloak the naked each time
In different attire and reverse
the flow on the riverbed? I remained

Practically speechless.

I don't know what they'll decide (if or when)
The authentic authors who try
The hearts and the rest of the organs;
Maybe they will ascribe dark sarcasm
Elegy disguised as satire
The word that hesitates ambiguous
On a tightrope —
It's inappropriate for me
To assume in this
What others might perhaps assume.

The only thing that worries me
(It doesn't worry me at all, I'm kidding)
Is that from all I've written
From that alone shall I be understood.
A well-known Cavafian line. And an axiom.
But more of a master-key for the critics
To unlock wide-open drawers, seeking out
Bringing effortlessly to light
The obvious. Conventions of a personal life

ΤΑ ΛΟΓΙΑ ΜΕΝΟΥΝ

Τοῦ περιβάλλοντος, τῆς ἐποχῆς. Πράξεις
Καί λόγια πού ἔφυγαν
Μένουν γιά πάντα, ὡς φαίνεται· νά μᾶς θυμίζουν.

Ποιές πράξεις ἀπ' τίς τόσες ἄραγε, ποιά λόγια;
Τό μόνο πού μέ ἀνησυχεῖ.

Ἀλλά ἴσως δέν ἀξίζει νά καταβληθεῖ
Τόση φροντίς καί τόσος κόπος νά μέ μάθουν.

Δέν ἀστειεύομαι.

Of the era, of the milieu. Deeds
And words that fled
Remain forever it seems; bringing us to mind.

Which deeds from the many, I wonder, which words?
That's all that worries me.

But maybe it isn't worth expending
So much care and effort to get to know me.

I am not kidding.

ΤΟ ΓΡΑΠΤΟ

Ἀρχίζοντας ἕνα γραπτό τί θέλουμε;
Νά μποῦμε στό κουκούτσι αὐτοῦ τοῦ κόσμου;
Ἤ νά τόν σπάσουμε;
Νά ἐξαχνωθεῖ στή φαντασία
Καί ἄφθαρτο
Ν' ἀναδυθεῖ ἕνα σύμπαν ἀπό λέξεις; Ἡ ἄμπωτη
Ν' ἀφήσει πίσω της κροκάλες αἰσθημάτων;
Φόβους καί ὄνειρα; (Τ' ἀπόνερα τοῦ ὕπνου ἐννοῶ.
Καί τ' ἄλλα, γιά τό αὔριο πού βαραίνει). Ἀρχίζοντας
Πάντα τό ἴδιο ἀτέλειωτο γραπτό
Μ' ἕνα ὀρμαθό
Ἀπό ρυθμούς καί εἰκόνες. Νιώθοντας
Πώς τίποτα δέν θέλουμε στ' ἀλήθεια — πώς
Ἕνα γραπτό εἶν' ἕνα σύμπαν ἀπό τίποτα. Καί πώς

Αὐτό τό ἀτέλειωτο γραπτό
Εἶναι τό γραφτό μας.

WRITING

What do we seek when we start writing?
To get inside the kernel of this world?
Or to break the world?
Make it sublimate into imagination
And have an indestructible
Universe of words emerge? Have the ebb tide
Leave behind the shingle of emotions?
Fears and dreams? (I mean the ripples of sleep.
And the rest, for the tomorrow that impends). Beginning
Always this same endless text
With a handful
Of rhythms and images. Sensing
That really we want nothing — that
A text is a universe made from nothing. And that

This endless writing
Is what has, for us, been written.

ΓΡΑΦΩ

Γράφω·
Ἔγραψα·
Ἔχω γράψει.

Καλά ὥς ἐδῶ.

Ὅμως τοῦ λείπει ὁ μέλλοντας.
Ἀδόκιμη ἡ προστακτική.
Κι ἡ ὁριστική του, εὐφημισμός
Τῆς εὐκτικῆς.

Ἀνώμαλο ρῆμα, ἐντέλει.
Περίπλοκο.

Ποιός μπορεῖ νά τό μάθει.

I WRITE

I write;
I wrote;
I've written.

It's fine so far.

But no Future tense.
Imperative invalid.
And the Indicative, a euphemism
Of the Optative.

An irregular verb, after all.
Complicated.

Who could ever learn it.

ΘΕΛΩ ΝΑ ΓΡΑΨΩ ΕΝΑ ΠΟΙΗΜΑ

Νά πλεύσει πάνω ἀπ' τά νερά πού θά 'ρθουνε
Νά σώσει αὐτό πού ἀναλώθηκε στή λήθη
Τό εὔθραυστο
Τό μαῦρο φωτεινό
Τόσο περίπλοκο κι ἁπλό
Τόσο ἀκατάληπτο
Πού μοιάζει ἀσάλευτα ἐδῶ ἐνῶ ἀναλήφθηκε
Σ' οὐράνιους θύλακες τοῦ νοῦ,
Πέτρα
Καί πούπουλο.
Ἕνα ποίημα τυφλό
Χωρίς ἀλφάβητο
Μεδούλι μεθυσμένο μές στά κόκαλα
Νά λέει χωρίς νά λέει κι ἀδούλωτο
Νά ρέει ὅλο θυμό ποτίζοντας
Μέ νόημα χωρίς νόημα καί ρυθμό
Αὐτό πού ἀθόρυβα
Γκρεμίστηκε στά σκότη.
                    Κάποτε
Θέλω νά γράψω ἕνα ποίημα μέ τίτλο:
«Θέλω νά γράψω ἕνα ποίημα».

I'D LIKE TO WRITE A POEM

To sail over the waters which are coming
To save that which oblivion has devoured
The fragile
The gleaming black
So complicated and so simple
So incomprehensible
Which seems stuck here though it's been taken up
Into celestial pockets of the mind,
Stone
And feather.
A blind poem
Without an alphabet
Marrow intoxicated inside the bones
To speak without speaking and unrestrained
To flow full of rage watering
With sense without sense or rhythm
That which without a sound
Has tumbled into darkness.
      One day
I'd like to write a poem with the title:
"I'd like to write a poem".

ΤΟ ΑΠΟΒΑΡΟ

Μιλᾶς μέ λέξεις.
Μεταφράζεις τό ἄγνωστο
Σέ κάτι πιό ἄγνωστο. Ἀνταλλάσσοντας
Τ' ἀσήκωτο τῆς ὕλης μ' ἕνα κίβδηλο
Χαρτοφυλάκιο
Γεμάτο ἄυλες μετοχές
Ἀντωνυμίες
Καί ῥήματα.

Ποιό χθόνιο λαρύγγι ἄραγε
Δίνει φωνή σ' ἕνα φωνῆεν;
Μέ ποιό στοιχεῖο αὐτοῦ τοῦ κόσμου
Συμφωνεῖ ἕνα σύμφωνο;

Μηδαμινές μπουκιές ἀέρα
Ὑποδύονται τέρατα. Σκέψου λοιπόν:
Γιά τόν ψαρά
Ἡ λέξη *δίχτυ* περιττεύει. Ἀτίθασα
Ἔμψυχα κι ἄψυχα ὁρμοῦν στίς σημασίες
Σαρώνοντας. Ποδοπατοῦν
Τό νόημα τῶν ὀνομάτων καί ἄηχα
(Τί ἐμπαιγμός! τρία ἠχηρά
φωνήεντα στό *ἄηχα*)
Σῶμα μέ σῶμα διεκδικοῦν
Ὅ,τι ὀνειρεύτηκαν πώς εἶναι. Μεταλλάσσοντας
Ἔξω ἀπό γλώσσα κι ἀπό σκέψη
Τό ἄγνωστο
Σέ κάτι ἀκόμα πιό ἐρεβῶδες.
Καί ἀσήκωτο.

Στό ἄυλο
Ἀπόβαρο
Τῆς ὕλης.

THE TARE-WEIGHT

You speak with words.
You translate the unknown
Into something more unknown. Exchanging
The unliftable weight of matter
For a forged portfolio
Full of immaterial assets, participles
Pronouns
And verbs.

Which chthonic larynx
Gives voice to a vowel?
To which element in this world
Does a consonant consent?

Trivial bites of air
Travesties of monsters. So think:
For the fisherman
The word *net* is redundant. Unruly
Animate and inanimate surge towards the meanings
Sweeping. Trample the
Meaning of names and soundlessly
(What a mockery! three resounding
vowels in *soundlessly*)
Going head-to-head they claim
Whatever it is they dreamt they were. Changing
Outside of language and of thought
The unknown
Into something more tenebrous.
And unliftable.

Into the immaterial
Tare-weight
Of matter.

ΤΟ ΚΕΛΙ

Ἔξω παφλάζουνε τά χρώματα τῆς μέρας
Σκέψεις αἰσθήματα χαράζουν τό κενό.
Κι ἐσύ κλεισμένος κλειδωμένος ἔγκλειστος
Στούς τέσσερις στίχους.

THE CELL

The colours of day rustle outside
Thoughts, emotions etch the void.
And you shut in, locked up, confined
Within four lines.

ΠΟΙΗΣΗ

Μεταφορές παρομοιώσεις κρέμονται
Σάν τάματα. Προσθέτω μία:

Ἐλιξήριο λέξεων.

POETRY

Metaphors similes hang
Like votive offerings. I'll add one more:

Lexical elixir.

ΤΟ ΠΟΙΗΜΑ

Ἀφοῦ κανένας ὁρισμός
Δέν εἶναι ὁριστικός
Κι ἀφοῦ ἀπ' τίς χίλιες ἐκδοχές
Καμιά δέν ἀπαντάει
    Τί νά 'ναι
    Ποίημα,
Φαντάζομαι δέν θά βαρύνουν
Τρεῖς ἀκόμα λέξεις:
    Ρυθμικά
    Σκεπτόμενο
    Αἴσθημα.

THE POEM

Since no definition
Is definitive
And since none of the thousand versions
Not one can say
    What a poem
    Might be,
I imagine three more words
Won't be a burden:
    Rhythmically
    Reflective
    Emotion.

ΟΙ ΠΟΙΗΤΕΣ

Μετά τό ποίημα
Οἱ ποιητές
Νιώθουν θλιμμένοι.

Ὅπως τά ζῶα
Μετά τόν ἔρωτα.

THE POETS

After the poem
The poets
Feel blue.

Like animals
After coition.

ΜΝΗΜΟΣΥΝΟ ΓΕΝΝΗΣΗΣ

Σήμερα, 22 Μαρτίου 2012,
Πού αὐτό τό ποίημα πάει νά γεννηθεῖ
— Καί πρίν ἀκόμα γεννηθεῖ —
Ἀναρωτιέμαι: ἄραγε
Σέ τρεῖς δεκαετίες ἀκριβῶς
22 Μαρτίου '42 ἀνήμερα
— Τό ποίημα θά 'ναι τότε ὀρφανό
Καί κουρασμένο —, ἄραγε
Θά ὑπάρξει κάποιος ἐπιζῶν πού θά σκεφτεῖ
Μιά τόσο ἀσήμαντη ἐπέτειο καί θ' ἀνοίξει
Ἐτούτη τή σελίδα πού διαβάζετε
Νά τή διαβάσει πάλι σιωπηλά
    Χαρίζοντας
Φιλί μιᾶς δεύτερης ζωῆς
Στίς τυπωμένες λέξεις —
    Ἤ ἀνάβοντας
Σάν τεθλιμμένος ἔστω συγγενής
Κεράκι ἐνθύμησης
    Στό μυστικό
    Μνημόσυνο
    Μιᾶς γέννησης;

MEMORIAL OF A BIRTH

Today, March 22nd, 2012,
This poem is about to be born
— And even before it is born —
I am wondering whether
In precisely three decades
On that day, March 22nd, '42
— The poem will be an orphan
And exhausted — whether
There will be any survivor to think
Of such a petty anniversary and open
This very page you are reading
To read it silently again
     Giving
The kiss of life
To the printed words —
     Or lighting
Like a grieving relative
A candle of remembrance
       At the mysterious
       Memorial
       Of a Birth?

NOTES

The purpose of these notes is to identify allusions to and quotations from the works of other authors. Each note begins with the page number of the English translation of the poem.

3. POETRY IS A NOBLE SHROUD
The title is a play on the words of Theodora, wife of Emperor Justinian, uttered during the Nika Revolt of AD 532, as reported by Procopius: ὡς καλὸν ἐντάφιον ἡ βασιλεία ἐστί. Procopius, *De bellis libri* I-IV, I.24: 37-38. The full quotation makes it clear that Theodora was aware that "noble shroud" was a metaphor that earlier authors had applied to things other than "imperial status" (βασιλεία, *vasileia*).

23. POETRY WITHIN POETRY, 2
Comme il pleure dans mon coeur ("As it weeps in my heart") Derived from a well-known poem by Paul Verlaine (1902, 155), but combining its first two lines: "Il pleure dans mon coeur / Comme il pleut dans la ville" ("It weeps in my heart / As it rains in the town"). The first line of Fostieris' poem may be compared with the second line of Verlaine's, with "a poem" replacing "the town".

49. POETRY WITHIN POETRY, 15
To thee I turn O art of poetry. The Greek is an exact quotation from a poem by C. P. Cavafy (1860–1930: line 5 of "Melancholy of Jason, son of Cleander, poet in Kommagene, A.D. 595" (Cavafy 2007, 130, 131). See also the note to pages 81, 83 below.

57. THAT THE POET MUST IF HE WOULD BE A POET
The title, in Ancient Greek, is a quotation from Plato. While in prison awaiting execution, Socrates had a dream that urged him to write poetry: "'Socrates,' it said, 'make music and work at it.'" (Plato, *Phaedo* 60e). In his attempt to obey the dream and compose poetry, Socrates turned one of Aesop's fables into verse, because he considered "that the poet must if he would be a poet compose fables but not speeches": Ὅτι τὸν ποιητὴν δέοι εἴπερ μέλλοι ποιητὴς εἶναι ποιεῖν μύθους ἀλλ' οὐ λόγους (*ibid.* 61b).

67. RIVER POEM
"It never turns back" invokes a well-known Greek rhyming riddle, Πάει πάει πάει καὶ δὲν γυρνάει. Τί εἶναι; Τὸ ποτάμι. "It goes it goes it

goes and turns not back. What is it?" — Answer: "A river".

"One cannot step into the same one [i.e. river] twice" translates Fostieris' adaptation of Heraclitus' fragment 91: Ποταμῷ γὰρ οὐκ ἔστιν ἐμβῆναι δὶς τῷ αὐτῷ (Diels 1934, 171).

73. METAPOETRY

"Can that come into being / which existed not before? [...] Impossible for that to perish which existed hitherto" is from Empedocles, fragments 11 and 12: νήπιοι οὐ γάρ σφιν δολιχόφρονές εἰσι μέριμναι, οἳ δὴ γίγνεσθαι πάρος οὐκ ἐὸν ἐλπίζουσιν ἢ τι καταθνήσκειν τε καὶ ἐξόλλυσθαι ἁπάντῃ. [...] τ' ἐὸν ἐξαπολέσθαι ἀνήνυστον καὶ ἄπυστον. In Gurthrie's translation (1965) this reads: "Fools — for they have no far-reaching thoughts, who suppose that what formerly was not can come into being, or that anything can die and perish wholly. [...] it cannot be brought about or heard of that what is should perish."

"Alcibiades [...] Dashed around at dawn cutting the balls / Off all the herms, making a eunuch of a god." Plutarch (*Alcibiades* 18–19), among other ancient authors, mentions that while the Athenian fleet was preparing to depart on the Sicilian expedition, some unpropitious signs appeared, among them the mutilation of the hermae (or herms), for which Alcibiades was accused by his arch enemy Androcles and other Athenians. Herms were statues consisting of the head (sometimes with the upper body) of the god Hermes on top of a square stone post, and some also had male genitalia projecting from the front of the post. While the ancient sources are not entirely clear about what happened, it is generally thought that the genitalia were knocked off as well as the faces being damaged.

"Fools though they hear / Be like unto the deaf" is from Heraclitus' fragment 34 (Diels 1934, 159), reproduced exactly in Fostieris' Greek. Compare Guthrie's translation (1962, 412).

77. POETRY IS NOT MADE WITH IDEAS

The title is an often-quoted remark by made by Stéphane Mallarmé to the painter Dégas, who had complained that he couldn't write poetry although he had many ideas. The original concludes "it is made with words." ("Ce n'est pas avec des idées qu'on fait des vers, c'est avec des mots" — Delacroix 1927, 92.)

"The intellect must first conceive and then the heart should feel with passion." These are the words of the poet Dionysios Solomos (1798–1857, author of the *Hymn to Liberty* which became the Greek National Anthem), as reported by his first editor Iakovos Polylas (1825–1896). Fostieries omits the end the sentence; the original reads

"... then the heart should feel what the mind conceived": Πρέπει πρῶτα μέ δύναμη νά συλλάβη ὁ νοῦς [...] κι ἔπειτα ἡ καρδιά θερμά νά αἰσθανθῆ ὅ,τι ὁ νοῦς ἐσυνέλαβε (Solomos 1961, 12).

81, 83. YOU ALWAYS EMERGE ALIVE FROM A POEM

"Fortunate dead" echoes the opening of Lorentzos Mavilis' sonnet "Oblivion" (Λήθη):"Fortunate the dead who forget / the bitterness of life" (Mavilis 1967, 135).

"And suicides / Ideal" evokes the title of a highly ironic poem, "Ideal Suicides" by Kostas Karyotakis (1896–1928), from his collection *Elegies and Satires*, published in 1927, the year before his own suicide (Karyotakis 1995, 114).

"On ailments / That lie in fantasy / And words" adapts lines from Cavafy's poem "Melancholy of Jason..." already cited above in connection with page 49. Addressing the "Art of Poetry" Jason says "you know something about soothing drugs; / attempts to numb the pain, in Imagery and Word" (Cavafy 2007, 130, 131). The Greek word *phantasia* can be translated as "fantasy", "imagination" or "imagery".

85, 87. THE SPOKEN WORDS REMAIN

"The authentic authors who try / The hearts and the rest of the organs" alludes to Psalm 7.9: "the righteous God trieth the hearts and reins [kidneys]" (Authorized Version, 1611). Fostieris makes the allusion clear by using the Ancient Greek participle ἐτάζοντες ("trying", "examining", "testing") from the Septuagint (the Greek translation of the Old Testament made before the Christian Era), where it is followed by the words (both Ancient and Modern Greek) for "hearts and kidneys": καρδίας καὶ νεφροὺς.

"*Only from that will I be understood*" and the two italicized lines on page 87 immediately preceding the final line are from Cavafy's poem "Hidden things", the original Greek reproduced exactly by Fostieris (Cavafy 1997, 92).

"*Of the era, of the milieu*" is from the last stanza of Karyotakis' poem "Altogether", an ironic, self-reflective poem about the poet and his art: "And if we roam all day starving / and if we spend the night under bridges / we were the scapegoats / of the "era", of the "milieu"" (Karyotakis 1995, 103).

BIBLIOGRAPHY

Barthes, Roland, 1972. *Critical Essays*, tr. Richard Howard. Evanston, IL: Northwestern University Press.

Beaton, Roderick, 1987. "From Mythos to Logos: The poetics of George Seferis", *Journal of Modern Greek Studies* 5.2, 135–152.

Beaugrade, Robert de, 1978. *Factors in a Theory of Poetic Translating*. Assen: Van Gorcum.

Benjamin, Walter, 1978. *Reflections*, tr. E. E. Jephcott, ed. Peter Demetz. New York: Harcourt Brace Jovanovitch.

Bloom, Harold, 1975. *A Map of Misreading*. Oxford: Oxford University Press.

―――― 1997. *The Anxiety of Influence*. Oxford: Oxford University Press.

Cavafy, C. P., 1997. Κ. Π. Καβάφης. *Κρυμμένα Ποιήματα 1877;–1923* [*Hidden Poems 1877?–1923*], ed. Γ. Π. Σαββίδης [G. P. Savidis]. Athens: Ikaros.

―――― 2007. *The Collected Poems*, tr. Evangelos Sachperoglou, ed. Peter Mackridge, Greek text ed. Anthony Hirst, Oxford World's Classics. Oxford: Oxford University Press.

Chrysanthopoulos, Michalis, 2012. Μιχάλης Χρυσανθόπουλος, *Ὁ Ἑλληνικός ὑπερρεαλισμός καὶ ἡ κατασκευή τῆς παράδοσης* [*Greek Surrealism and the Construction of the Tradition*]. Athens: Agra.

Delacroix, Henri, 1927. *La Psychologie de l'art*. Paris: F. Alcan.

Derrida, Jacques, 1980. *Writing and Difference*, tr. Alan Bass. London: Routledge.

―――― 1997. *Of Grammatology*. Baltimore, MD: Johns Hopkins University Press.

Diels, H. 1934 (and later editions and reprints). *Die Fragmente deer Vorsokratiker Griechisch und Deutsch*, ed. W. Kranz, 5th edn, vol. 1. Berlin: Weidmann.

Elytis, Odysseas, 1987. Ὀδυσσέας Ἐλύτης, *Ἀνοιχτά Χαρτιά* [*Open Papers*]. Athens: Ikaros.

Fostieris, Andonis, 1971. Ἀντώνης Φωστιέρης, *Τό Μεγάλο Ταξίδι* [*The Great Journey*]. Athens: private edition.

―――― 1977. Ἀντώνης Φωστιέρης, *Σκοτεινός Ἔρωτας* and *Ποίηση μές στήν Ποίηση* [*Dark Eros* and *Poetry within Poetry*]. Athens: Kedros.

―――― 1981. Ἀντώνης Φωστιέρης, *Ὁ διάβολος τραγούδησε σωστά* [*The Devil sang in tune*]. Thessaloniki: Egnatia.

―――― 1984. *The Devil Sang in Tune* and *Dark Eros*, tr. Kimon Friar, Contemporary Poets Series. San José, CA: Realities Library.

―――― 1987. Ἀντώνης Φωστιέρης, *Τό θά καί τό νά τοῦ θάνατος* [*The D and A of Death*]. Athens: Kastaniotis.

Fostieris, Andonis, 1996. Ἀντώνης Φωστιέρης, *Ἡ σκέψη ἀνήκει στό πένθος* [*Thought Belongs to Mourning*]. Athens: Kastaniotis.

——— 2003. Ἀντώνης Φωστιέρης, *Πολύτιμη Λήθη* [*Precious Oblivion*] Athens: Kastaniotis.

——— 2009. Anthony Fostieris, *Precious Oblivion*, tr. Thom Nairn and Dionysia Zervanou. Edinburgh: Dionysia Press.

——— 2013. Ἀντώνης Φωστιέρης, *Τοπία τοῦ Τίποτα* [*Landscapes of Nothingness*]. Athens: Kastaniotis.

——— 2020. Ἀντώνης Φωστιέρης, *Θάνατος ὁ Δεύτερος* [*Second Death*]. Athens: Kastaniotis.

——— 2021. Ἀντώνης Φωστιέρης, *Ἅπαντα τά Ποιήματα 1970–2020* [*Complete Poems 1970–2020*]. Athens: Kastaniotis.

Guthrie, W. K. C., 1962. *A History of Greek Philosophy*, vol. 1: *The Earlier Presocratics and the Pythagoreans*. Cambridge: Cambridge University Press.

——— 1965. *A History of Greek Philosophy*, vol. 2: *The Presocratic tradition from Parmenides to Democritus*. Cambridge: Cambridge University Press, 1965.

Hirst, Anthony, 2004. *God and the Poetic Ego: the Appropriation of Biblical and Liturgical Language in the Poetry of Palamas, Sikelianos and Elytis*. Bern: Peter Lang.

Holmes, James S., 1988. *Translated! Papers on Literary Translation*. Amsterdam: Rodopi.

Jakobson, Roman, 1949. "The Phonemic and Grammatical Aspects of Language in their Interrelations", *Proceedings of the Sixth International Congress of Linguists*, ed. M. Lejeune, 5–18. Paris: Klincksieck.

——— 1981. "Linguistics and poetics", *Selected Writings* vol. 3: *Poetry of Grammar and Grammar of Poetry*, ed. Stephen Rudy, 18–51. The Hague: Mouton.

——— 1985. "Closing Statement: Linguistics and Poetics", *Semiotics: an Introductory Anthology*, ed. R. E. Innis, 145–175. Bloomington, IN: Indiana University Press.

Karyotakis, K. G. 1995. Κ. Γ. Καρυωτάκης, *Ποιήματα καί Πεζά* [*Poems and Prose Writings*], ed. Γ. Π. Σαββίδης [G. P. Savidis]. Athens: Estia.

Lautréamont, Comte de (Isidore Lucien Ducasse) 1981. «Ποιήματα» ["Poems"], tr. Ἀντώνης Φωστιέρης [Andonis Fostieris], *Ἡ Λέξη* 1, (January 1981), 28–33.

——— 1990. *Les Chants de Maldoror*. Paris, Flammarion.

Lloyd, Rosemary, 1999. *Mallarmé: The Poet and his Circle*. New York: Cornell University Press.

Loulakaki-Moore, Irene, 2010a. *Seferis and Elytis as Translators*. Bern: Peter Lang.

——— 2010b. "Precious Poetry", *Athens News*, 8–14 January 2010, 30.

Loulakaki-Moore, Irene, 2013. "The metaphysics of darkness: three rhymed poems by Andonis Fostieris", *iNTERCULTURAL tRANSLATION iNTERSEMIOTIC* (E Journal) 2.1.

——— 2014. "The Dark Philosopher and the postmodern turn: Heraclitus in the poetry of Seferis, Elytis and Fostieris", *Byzantine and Modern Greek Studies* 38.1, 91–113.

——— 2018a. "Poesia nella Poesia — La Musa pensante", *Poesia* 336, 12–13.

——— 2018b. *"Poetry within Poetry*: the thinking muse", *Modern Greek Studies Online / Journal of the Society of Modern Greek Studies* 4, 7–13.

Lyotard, J.-F., 1992. "Answering the question: What is Postmodernism?", *The Post-modern Reader*, ed C. Jencks, 138–150. London: Academy Editions; New York: St Martin's Press.

Mavilis, Lorentzos 1967. Λορέντζος Μαβίλης, Άπαντα [*Complete Works*]. Athens: Maris Editions.

McGinn, Colin, 1993. *Problems in Philosophy: The Limits of Inquiry*. Oxford: Blackwell.

Murray, Penelope, 2002. "Plato's Muses: the Goddesses that endure", *Cultivating the Muse: Struggles for Power and Inspiration in Classical Literature*, ed. Efrossini Spentzou and Don Fowler, 29–46. Oxford: Oxford University Press.

Nietzsche, Friedrich, 1968. *The Will to Power*, tr. W. Kaufmann and R. J. Hollingdale, ed. W. Kaufmann. New York: Vintage Books.

Rorty, R., 1989. *Contingency, Irony and Solidarity*, Cambridge: Cambridge University Press.

Seferis, George, 1974. Γιώργος Σεφέρης, *Ποιήματα* [*Poems*], 9th edn. Athens: Ikaros.

——— 1995. *Collected Poems*, tr. Edmund Keeley and Philip Sherrard, revised edn. Princeton: Princeton University Press.

Solomos, Dionysios, 1961. Διονύσιος Σολωμός, Άπαντα [*Complete Works*], vol. 1: *Ποιήματα* [*Poems*], ed. Λίνος Πολίτης [Linos Politis]. Athens: Ikaros.

Thomasson, Amie, 2009. "Answerable and Unanswerable Questions", *Metametaphysics: New Essays on the Foundations of Ontology*, ed. D. Chalmers, D. Manley and R. Wassermann, 444–471. Oxford: Oxford University Press,.

Valéry, Paul, 1957. *Oeuvres*, vol. 1, Paris: Gallimard.

——— 1960. *Oeuvres*, vol. 2. Paris: Gallimard.

Van Dyck, Karen, 1998. *Kassandra and the Censors: Greek Poetry since 1967*. Ithaca, NY: Cornell University Press.

Verlaine, Paul, 1902. *Oeuvres Complètes*, vol. 1. Paris: Vanier.

Wittgenstein, Ludwig, 1953. *Philosophical Investigations*. Oxford: Blackwell.